Life:

FROM GENERATION Z

Life:
FROM GENERATION Z

Lane Farrell

ARCHWAY
PUBLISHING

Archway Publishing books may be ordered
through booksellers or by contacting:

Archway Publishing
1663 Liberty Drive
Bloomington, IN 47403
www.archwaypublishing.com
1 (888) 242-5904

All Scripture quotations are taken from the King James Version.

ISBN: 978-1-4808-8429-8 (sc)
ISBN: 978-1-4808-8430-4 (e)

Library of Congress Control Number: 2019917147

Print information available on the last page.

Archway Publishing rev. date: 11/06/2019

Contents

Introduction

GENERATION Z IS BY FAR THE MOST IM-
pressionable generation there has ever been. With the
constant bickering between millennials and older generations, a wake of confusion exists along the path for
Generation Z. Amid this confusion, core values are
being reinterpreted and fitted to satisfy the needs of
an ever-changing society. Consequently, Generation Z
is left isolated, having to determine their own value
structure based on a portrayal of two opposing forces
that derive from the new and old waves.

For obvious reasons, one can point toward social
media as the source of the new wave of a generation.
Ultimately, this has become so true to the point that it
is nearly driving the existence of many people toward
ideas and groups rather than individual thought. As a
result, those who are not strong enough to deal with
the world in its raw form begin to hide within the false

security of social media, finding themselves crippled to the point of serious mental health issues.

Social media has created a viable means of opportunity for many individuals to better their lives. With that said, social media can also greatly hinder the ability of individuals to correctly discover who they are. Social media has an intriguing similarity to any other form of addiction; it makes the individual obsess over the necessity to have access to constant stimuli of gratification. When the stimuli are not present, the individual is hopeless. In many ways, the collective personality that has come about as a result of social media has also become entirely reflective of the morality of Generation Z.

With morals being redefined to fit the needs of society, it is incredibly hard for Generation Z to surmount the obstacles in front of them without being able to understand the world for what it truly is. Unfortunately, it will become increasingly hard for them to do so if they are kept within the pitfall of confusion that is associated with following the path of outdated means of living. Generation Z needs new stimuli. They are unfit to go "cold turkey" in regards to their prior means of living, but they must become more enlightened to the point that they can find a new stimulus within a meaningful existence.

In life, there must be moral guidelines, predicated around one's own comprehension of philosophical principles. Generation Z needs such guidelines to move them away from conflict and toward the direction of competence and understanding. This is the reason for me embarking upon writing this work: to create guidelines for Generation Z, from Generation Z, in the hopes of creating a productive group of young individuals who have a sense of meaning to adhere by.

A connection cannot be made without trust. This is why the generations before now have slowly started to fail the current generation. We have no reason to believe that the older generations are valid when they are swindling us into accepting their words of "truth" while segregating us into groups based on our identity. There is no individualism. When you take away individualism, you take away the means for trust to exist in the world.

A new wave of people will certainly come out of Generation Z. The common belief that is tied to Generation Z is that they are incompetent and carry a sense of entitlement with them. The image must be changed, and I do believe that I have something to offer on behalf of Generation Z. The information that I am providing was known for hundreds of years by philosophers, psychologists, and literary minds, but it seems to have been recently lost. My aim is for people to become in touch with a side of themselves that they have never seen before. This can only be done if they embark upon discovering the mechanisms of the world and by interacting with people in a manner that is the best fit not only for existence but for life.

Life is understood through discovery. Confusion

will lead to pain after time, but through this pain, one discovers that life is only temporary and must be utilized wherever it is given. The value of such a discovery is that one learns that sacrifice is a means of sustenance. The idea at hand is one of the principal virtues that I learned after many of my own struggles. To be able to put your own struggles behind you to search for a greater means of existence in the lives of whom one cares about: that is the greatest of all things.

Writing this book was greatly predicated upon the idea of placing my own insecurities and hardships in the past as a means to help those who are experiencing something existentially similar. I hope that you will have the opportunity to discover something about yourself in this book that you have never encountered before. Now is the time for you to understand that of which is most important.

Chapter 1

Change and Why It Is Important

IF YOU WANT CHANGE, MAKE IT HAPPEN. Relationships, outlooks, passions—these are all things that, given an active effort, will soon unfold in your life. It is too often seen that people continually complain over abstract ideas, those over which they do not have any power. In the age of social media, it seems much easier to go on Twitter quoting Drake lyrics in the hopes of somebody direct messaging us to cheer us up. After we have done this for the umpteenth time, we begin to realize a pattern, and we look up and realize how pathetic we really are. When we have realized the pattern, it is clear to us that the only person capable of creating change is ourselves.

I am not trying to lessen the severity of anyone's situation by saying this, and in many ways, I am only trying to make people more socially conscious, but I do believe we deserve a large number of our problems simply because we have been taught to act in a way in which we expect others to do our work for us. Complaints without a proper cause of action will keep you static. It is often difficult and tiresome to keep battling through situations that seem to repeat themselves, but it is this process that makes life worth living. Experiencing the same results, especially those that do not benefit us, reveals to us one of the greatest contributors into the overall teachings of mental resilience. I have yet to meet an individual who has received everything they wished for without working toward it. People can get away with this at most a couple of times before the universal law of failure comes into play. It is only at the moment when we can control that of which is in our grasp that things not in our immediate vicinity will begin to change. Expecting to change things without having a sufficient means of doing so is an absurdity. Small things make big things happen, similar to a snowball effect.

It took me years to finally sit down and assess what exactly it was that I wanted to do in regards to creating a book. After deleting many copies of former ideas I had, I realized that I had created a purposeless pattern of action because I never acted on the will to follow through. So here we are. Perhaps this is exactly how it must be. Before, I kept on telling myself to wait until I could be taken seriously in this world as an author. There is no time for that. We will soon be dead, and all the dreams we wished to have aspired toward will die with us. Noticing the patterns that I had a propensity to follow allowed me to understand exactly how necessary it was for me to change the course of action I was on.

People often contrive the idea in their minds that worthwhile change is this vast, esoteric realm which the thousands will never feel. And it is with this thought that I say to them, "It is time to reassess who you are as a human being." Change, no matter how small, is a vital aspect of being and must be valued.

The following are my attempts at enacting sufficient means of change:

1. **Take time to go through your life and redefine that about which you were so formerly certain**. In most occasions, you may even realize that what you previously believed was entirely fallacious. We are often taught to believe that whatever the teacher, the preacher, the father, and the mother says must be valid. In many cases, what they say may be true, but they will never be entirely truthful to us all the time. Humans are not perfect beings, and hence, their actions are fallible. Nothing in life is absolute; therefore, things are always subject to change.

2. **Do not be so mindful all the time**. Yes, it is important to be aware, but when we are fixated on these indoctrinated beliefs that are unproven, we are simply wasting time. Discover the truth

that lies in the world, and then focus your mind. Never focus your mind on something that is inherently false.

3. **Understand what it is that you want in life.** We often want things that are not always going to be the most beneficial reward for us. Become comfortable in the idea of avoiding things that we only want to do rather than what we need to do.

4. **Understand what it is that you *need* in your life.** I am a firm believer that besides the basic necessities of human life, we must be highly dependent on that of which we feel morally obligated to do. Most of the things that we need are things that we feel we must do, and this idea of "must" stems from moral obligation.

It would be foolish of me to assert that these are the only proper ways of making a change in your life. In many ways, the ideas that I have listed off are meant to be scrutinized and rearranged to fit one's needs. With that said, I do believe that once a form of change has occurred in our lives, we will truly be able to understand its importance as long as we are no longer willfully blind to the self-evident truths of the social apparatus in which we exist.

Part of understanding the need for change has to do with how one interprets what is of value to them. Having a value structure one can frequently refer to is important to depict what form of change is most beneficial to our identity. I do believe that a value structure is a supreme foundation upon which one can build a life of meaningful intent.

Chapter 2

Understanding Your Identity

LIVING LIFE BASED ON THE OPINIONS OF others is one of the most crippling but frequent fallacies that people are often taught. Yes, it is good to consider the thoughts that other people have of you, but it should not be the basis of how you live. We all wish to appeal to the eyes of our peers, but I do believe that the only proper way to do so is to live our lives based on our own identities.

Understanding our identities can be difficult, for examining our life is often hard when we wish to impress others. The starting point for being able to examine one's identity is learning to neglect any preconceived limiting beliefs that either our mind or the thoughts of others have attempted to contain us within. From there, we can journey toward understanding exactly who we are.

Upon entering a state of absolute self-discovery, it is imperative to look back on past experiences and generalize them as best as we can. For instance, when formulating questions as a means of examination, ask yourself, "Am I somebody who enjoys company over solitude?" rather than a question such as, "At that party last weekend, was I overly antisocial?" The reason for generalizing your questions is quite simple: our current state of affairs will often attempt to blind us to how we actually feel. Depression is the foremost example of an inner condition that may skew how we look at ourselves on an existential level of importance. Continue to ask yourself these questions of an arbitrary nature. The questions you ponder over can be entirely rudimentary, for all that matters is that you are taking the initiative to understand yourself on a level of being that you would have never done so otherwise.

It is important to routinely ask yourself questions of such caliber because it allows you to stray away from inner conflict when put into situations with a greater amount of stress. If we are used to constantly scrutinizing our own thoughts, consequently, we will be prepared for most of the trials that come our way.

Understanding our identities will allow us to regard what is of a superior level of importance to us. Knowing the inner workings of our identity will allow us to see in physicality what we feel so inclined to do. In my personal experience, I have found that the omnipresent force on which I aim to build my life around is the existence of love, in all forms applicable. I was only able to come to this conclusion when I understood the great amount of pain and suffering that those closest to me constantly endured. My understanding of the need for pain and suffering led me into the direction of the belief that love—as clichéd as it may possibly be comprehended—is what unites us all. For me, understandably realizing that a great amount of my identity correlated with love, I was able to actively contribute into the lives of those whom I cared about most. Ultimately,, through this realization, I was even able to lessen the disparity that existed between the love I had for those dearest to me versus the love of my fellow man.

Many things become self-evidently true to us when we reach a point of superior comprehension of our inherent identity. With all things, the realization of what we identify with also leads us to see where we tend to stray toward malevolence. You cannot allow this to discourage you, for malevolence—as I will go more into depth later—is a structure that will always exist in life and will therefore always find ways to reconstitute itself. Rather than looking at our interactions with malevolence as disgraceful, be able to see that it is necessary to commit faults on occasion so that we may stray back onto the path where we desire to be. The beauty in this "path" idea that I have mentioned is that it is entirely something of our creation, something found in cooperation with identity.

Our shortcomings must not be the region where our hope dwindles. If this is the case, our hope will eventually cease to exist. For so long, I prided myself on being a just man, somebody in whom others could confide. After a while, I became used to this static state of helping others, and I also began to realize that there are instances when it may even be better to leave people to themselves. Taking this as quite an ego blow, I felt defeated. I started to have a lack of trust in the ideas of virtue that I discussed with friends. It finally hit me that I was throwing a pity party, hiding from the reality of life, wherein exists the structural body of agonizing, and impenetrable defeat, which always lingers.

Seeing the areas where we tend to crack under pressure is necessary because it is representative of distinct areas of our identity. Being fully aware of the places where we struggle the most can either help us improve in the given aspects or help us see the situations that we must avoid altogether. For instance, if you are a person who is prone to addiction, it would be wise to stay away from drugs and other substances, understanding these may lead you to an area where you wish not to stay. I say to you, own your shortcomings and fully accept all the terrible things you have done. Humans are fallible. We are fragile and often susceptible to failure. Having the ability to look back upon our wrongdoings will greatly contribute to identity awareness.

This idea eventually came to me after a long period of self-discovery: perhaps it is more enjoyable when we notice these things, the positive and negative aspects of our identity. For so long, I was looking for something much greater, but then I realized that all along, it was something inherent; it had been with me since the beginning. Although I did have to do extensive research—primarily dealing with examinations of personal development—in the means of discovering "it," "it" was always there, and this something greater, this "it," was my identity. The one thing that could keep me on the path that I needed, the one thing that would allow me to realize where I had fallen short of being morally just. It was all within me the entire time.

Understanding that "it" exists within you—your identity and the effects it has on the ability to change—is the introductory moment by which we step onto the path toward living fully. Living fully is taking life in as its most glorious and desirable form. The structure of our identities is something of an utterly unfathomable design because, usually, it is not something that anyone else can fully comprehend by knowing someone. I have, for a long time, been proud of the fact that no one will ever be able to understand who I truly am. How I am constantly thinking in words and ideas. How I will let people into my heart, but will never allow them to enter my mind and understand its complexities. Perhaps that is the most beautiful thing of all—the fact that only you understand your identity and only you can decide the degree to which you aim for others to know about you.

Essentially, understanding your identity can be experimented upon using these three questions: (1) What do I identify with? (2) Whom do I identify with? (3) Why do I identify with these people and characteristics?

Chapter 3

Goals, Dreams, Aspirations

I BELIEVE THAT PART OF WHAT SEPARATES us from each other in this world is the existence of goals in an individual's life. It is not always the case that those who have goals become successful and that those who are pessimistic go on to become less successful. I think it is entirely more complicated than that, mainly because a motivated person can always hope and pray, but if they do not put forth an effort, they will not get anywhere. My father is a wise man, perhaps one of the wisest I have met in my short time on this earth. He once told me that you can pray that you win the lottery as much as you want, but unless you play the lottery, you will never win. Contrived and simple but insightful nevertheless.

The majority of people who are looking to pursue their dreams are typically already putting the work in to do so. I simply thought it was necessary to distinguish the difference between dreaming alone and dreaming with a purposeful dedication. I think it is important to set goals, and in that respect, I advise you to set goals. Figuring out what you want in life is immensely important. Doing so will add another form of structure to your life that was previously non-existent.

Setting goals can be quite simple: decipher whatever it is you want and chase after it. Although there is not necessarily a right or wrong way to set goals, I would strongly advise you to go after what you need rather than what you want. There is a large disparity between what we need and what we want, and often it is a telltale sign of maturity when one can discern between the two. A common example of this is when we see people who have recently exited a relationship, thus becoming depressed and consequently desiring to have their partner back. They hold the conviction that getting back together with the person who once made them happy would be a surefire way of rediscovering happiness. This is the wrong indoctrination. I would advise you never to do something based on the idea that it is going to make you happy. Giving a depressed person happiness is an absurdity; the happiness will go away after a while, and they will end up in exactly the same place where they were before. Therefore, in the case of the individual who has been depressed after a breakup, I would say it would be most beneficial to them to set their goals based on their need to understand the world a little better than before. Truth and meaning are some of the most important things that one will come across in life. Truth and meaning will never be able to abandon you once they have been discovered.

It is important to differentiate between the magnitude of the goals that we pursue. For example, maybe it is not always the best thing to have one dream that is at the pinnacle of our efforts. It is often better to have multiple dreams of lesser importance. Smaller ambitions will add up after a while, and it will be the same as if you obtained one overarching dream. In my eyes, it is better to have a big goal that is simultaneously comprised of many other micro-ambitions.

Once you have created a plan that lists your aspirations, keep your head straight forward on the goal, and only let the small micro-ambitions that you have set aside get in the way. Do not let fear of failure get in your way. Failure is a self-evident truth of life; along with chaos, it will always find a way to reconstitute itself in another dimension of your life. Every goal is a longshot, but everybody loves a Rocky story. Be your own Rocky story. Have the mentality that someday, people are going to make major motion pictures of your life. Although it is slightly comical, it is a great mindset to have, largely because it is ambiguous. I have always believed that a life of ambiguity is better than a life of absolute structure. In that respect, do not be discouraged if your goals take longer to achieve than anticipated. Nothing is ever as we expect it to be. Life has a funny way of working itself out that way. Although, this is exactly how it should be. For instance, people often dream of having relations with somebody, praying to God only to find out that the person could not be more contrary to the characteristics of their identity. This is a contrived example, but I can nearly guarantee that you have seen a similar occurrence of this nature along a different dimension of your life—wishing for something only to see, after the fact, that it was something that you could have happily done without.

Another aspect needed to properly decipher the eminent value of a goal is the assessment of intent after carrying out the dream. In simpler terms, what is it you wish to achieve as a result of pursuing the dream? If you are only pursuing something because you believe it will make you more popular or simply because you want more attention, you are pursuing something while having the wrong intentions. There is an interesting quote in the Bible that I came across when researching archetypal themes in order to write this book. The words hold great weight, especially for the aforementioned idea I introduced: "But when thou doest alms, let not thy left hand know what thy right hand doeth" (Matthew, 6:3 KJV). Faith is something that will be discussed later in this book, although I do not believe that to understand the given words, you need to have any previous interference with the word of God or with religion in its entirety. In simpler terms, this Scripture can be understood in the twenty-first century as meaning it is better to do things for the sake of one's individual satisfaction rather than for the fame or publicity for having done so. Take these words for what they are, mere suggestions, similar to the ideas I have discussed. So, analogous to the Scripture, in terms of whatever goals you have in life, pursue them not so that the person next to you envies you but because it was of your own doing, of your will, that which feels obligated to do the things that are needed to sustain a beneficial existence on this earth.

The beauty in the struggle of pursuing goals is that it is something you can do entirely alone. Years down the line, you will have a family of your own, with little time on your hands to accomplish the things you desire to carry out. For the time being, appreciate every slightest bit of solitude you are able to have. I promise you, your future self will thank you for taking the lonely path into the unknown, preemptively defeating the desire of the self to be coddled by the chaotic nature of the group setting.

Ambitions are a glorious thing. Ambitions drive existence, mainly because they give people a purpose. Purpose is one of the most valued aspects of mental fortitude. Therefore, I wish for you to genuinely set goals, methodically and sensibly.

On the road to obtaining our goals, there will be manifold tribulations in the way. Do not become discouraged when you are knocked down from a plateau of superior movement toward a goal. You must knowingly go into every endeavor in life fully aware that a terrible amount of tragedy and suffering can be associated with aiming your goals higher than most. There is a certain amount of risk correlated with everything we do in life, and often, it is proportional to the magnitude of the goal; they are dependent on each other, existing upon the same plane. However, it is necessary to tell yourself that all the risks you face are mere trivialities compared to the goals that are established, further reinforcing why you must follow through and manifest what you want.

We are not perfect, and to believe we are would be ill-advised, although I have often pondered this idea of perfection. A long while ago, I decided that I would start making "perfect" goals in my mind, meaning that if all went as planned, the way I wished, that is how my goal would turn out. This idea is quite compelling, and it leaves us with a sense of hope. I do believe that creating goals of a perfect or idealized manner is representative of one's passion that they carry with them in both hobbies they are ambitious about and tasks that they resent doing. Using this structure of goal-setting has allowed me to plan out my life so I have a sense of urgency, although I would discourage one who is easily discouraged from using this process. Those who are easily discouraged may see the severe limits to their shortcomings when their goal has not been obtained because the perfect goal will never happen; chaos will always stand in the way of reaching perfection. It is one of the most important aspects of goal-setting to be able to understand that your goal may not occur, and given that you experience failure, recognize it as a step forward—possibly in the wrong direction—and continue to move forward through your own conviction. Use the idea that you may come up short to push you to a limit that you have never exceeded before.

Everything that happens to us in life should be looked at as a reason that our dreams are possible. Our dreams will be obtained after we have given an active effort to manifest what we want through the trials and tribulations that we must endure. There is no greater honor of self than when one has transcended out of chaos onto the path of achievement.

I live my life based on this saying, which I thought up. I hope it can be of use to you: "I walk onto a path of existence, that which no man has endured thus far."

Chapter 4
Tragedy and Suffering

THERE ARE TWO GREAT MALEVOLENT structural bodies in this world that tower over all other forms of evil. Tragedy and suffering lie at the pinnacle of all evil transfixed on the inhabitants of earthly matters. If we look at figures like Adolf Hitler, Eric Harris, or Jeffrey Dahmer, we see that there was a great want for these individuals to plunge the world into greater evil. Upon further inspection, we see, however, that most of the vile creatures that we have ever seen in the media or throughout history were all products of an environment of great structural evil. Nobody is born evil, although nobody is born good. We are placed in a world somewhere between malevolence and virtue, where all is doomed to fail if the will of beings is not prioritized. Because nobody can be inherently evil, we must turn to the conditions of their being, such as environmental conditions and social apparatuses during youth.

For so long, I was trying to comprehend how one person could have gone so wrong in their life that they could commit such atrocities. We see that the minds of these men begin to move more toward evil when great tragedy and suffering have found a foothold in their lives. The two bodies reconstitute themselves across dimensions, preying upon the minds of men who are weak in will and awareness. Perhaps part of the reason I truly wanted to write this book was to show people that not much separates good people from bad people, except for a few minor occurrences that begin to build on each other. A just individual and a malevolent person are born into the same world, but the environmental conditions that they are placed into, in cooperation with the social apparatus that they are entangled within, can produce two greatly different individuals, predicated on the presence of tragedy and suffering.

Having prior knowledge of the ideas at hand, maybe it is best to define tragedy and suffering and go on to establish their causes as well as repercussions. Tragedy exists in many forms, and it may even differ between two individuals, based on how receptive they are to the problems they face in life. Furthermore, tragedy is any calamity—physical, psychological, or emotional— that creates a sense of existing pain or sorrow in those susceptible to it. The response to tragedy, suffering, is defined as the feelings and effects, either long term or short term, that loom over the victim of malevolence.

Often, people wish not to discuss the depressing

side to life because they would rather look at everything with a sense of tunnel vision, blinding out everything that they wish not to see. I find this absurd because, truly, we are all united by tragedy, and the only guarantee in life is death. But there is great validity in this argument, because I believe that once we have understood how tragedy and suffering work and how they affect the human psyche, we can live our lives to the fullest because we are being truthful to ourselves. Happiness cannot be found without a sense of meaning, and if you truly believe that if all you ever do is walk through the world with tunnel vision, I pray for you, my friend, because there is a lot of hurt coming your way, and it is coming fast. Comprehension of evil is what liberates us; seeing where we go wrong in life can show us how to anticipate malevolence so that we can live happily.

It is often best to classify tragedy as being a form of destruction, for it usually meddles in the occurrence of death, failure, and ruination. Comprehending the matter as such is quite clever, because it is hard to simply put a complex structural body into a few words, and it is often better to think of the matter as it pertains to us, and the same goes for suffering.

The greatest tragedy that I have faced in life has been the death of one of my dearest friends (I wish to keep his name unmentioned out of respect for the family). He was a man who taught me so much, specifically on ideas relating to dreams and ambition, and I had a long period of drawn-out suffering after his death.

Although, looking back, it was this defining moment in my life that allowed me to understand the processes and the wrongdoings of the great evil energy that is inherent in life.

We will never be able to understand exactly how tragedy works because it is too complex in nature—being redefined from person to person—to ever truly grasp in one actual idea. On the other hand, suffering is something that can be understood easily, and the reconstitution of the evil that exists within suffering is an idea that needs to be taught and understood properly. Many times we see people who become depressed mainly because they have allowed their suffering to become more nourishing to them than any other aspect of their life. I am not speaking of those who are clinically depressed, because the two ideas exist in different dimensions.

People who have succumbed to their suffering to the point of being depressed can be helped only when they have understood the idea that their experiences are no more tragic than anybody else on this earth. The pain in our hearts felt after a tragedy is inherent, but it is what we do with our lives after the tragedy that allows us to neglect what it is that was hurting us so much. My friend who passed away was someone who meant the world to so many, and I speak for many when I say that we all felt the tremendous pain on the inside after his death. For a week after his death, I stood in my room in a state of severe depression, trying to find a means of genuine understanding. I believe that, in the occurrence of death, all we can bring to those affected is a sense of understanding and insight into why tragedy is important.

Tragedy is an intricate idea to wrap the mind around, for it is often unexpected. It usually occurs as such: life is going great, you recently married the love of your life, who is pregnant with your child, and then a month goes by, and it turns out that the baby is stillborn. These things happen, and they are so hard to comprehend because we come to the conclusion that in a world of moral virtue, it would not make any rational sense for such a tragedy to occur, but it must. As contrived as it may sound, perhaps every time somebody carries out an act of lasting virtue (for instance, donating a million dollars to a charity) then, quite literally, somebody will die. This goes back to the most primordial understanding from centuries ago: for every baby that was born, someone had to die. Certainly, this is still the case today, but our population is increasing disproportionately to the number of people who are dying. We are often shaped by tragedy, but we must not allow ourselves to turn into creatures of evil intent. We can avoid this by associating with groups that allow us to see the good in the world. Tragedy can be a hard thing to deal with, but we must deal with it, because if we allow it to take ownership over us, we establish a proclivity that leans toward doing wrong.

I urge you to throw yourself into the path of tragedy and suffering at least once in your life and confront them. There is great wisdom that can be obtained by understanding the presence of evil as a way to keep order in the world.

For parents and children alike, the loss of innocence is the first superior form of tragedy that takes place in a family dynamic. Whether this is the temptation of substance or the sometimes dangerous lust for a partner, it is a self-evident truth of life that maturity can often become a great tragedy. The repercussions of this are often seen as one thinking they have been subordinated into a state that prioritizes rebellion and angst over all other suitable forms of moral expression. Often it is the events of the teenage years, so full of raw emotion and angst, that are hotspots for the existence of malevolence to take place. Teenagers often fantasize about the idea of escaping the defined social apparatus in which they exist. There is a continual longing to get away from the brutalities of the world; however, running away from tragedy only makes you more prone to suffering later on. It is often the case that adolescents stray further away from their previous environment of constant parental supervision to a place where they keep parents from understanding the issues that they face. There seems to be an innate inferiority complex, especially since teenagers are generally more emotionally vulnerable than the rest of the population.

Seeing the real world in all of its brutalities and dimensional forms of reconstituted evil is important. In many ways, it is necessary to understand that there simply could not be an emergence of happiness in the world without the omnipresent universal forces of evil. It is best to comprehend the idea as the embodiment of darkness and light within the conditions that surround us, which is entirely related to the concept of yin and yang. Happiness could not exist without malevolence, for it is the feeling we experience when we transcend out of agony and other such evil structural bodies.

If we can find a way to predicate our existence into the foundations of spiritual equilibrium, where structural bodies such as evil and virtue can both be found in even amounts, we can live a life full of choice. I do believe that it is seeing the worst in the world that allows us to discover the best that the world has to offer.

> Remember that misfortunes come from
> God, and that men are never to blame.
> —Leo Tolstoy, *War and Peace*

Chapter 5

Depression and Mental Illness

FEELING UNSAFE IN ONE'S OWN MIND may be one of the greatest tragedies an individual may face. I have always believed that our minds should be the safest place that we can resort to in this world, in hopes of finding a means to end whatever issues we are facing. As I observed, however, I witnessed how this idea was constantly challenged, predominantly by the emotions of the teenage psyche. But why is this so? Perhaps we will never be able to truly get down to the bottom of why depression is so omnipresent, particularly in teenagers, although it is largely in part to individuals being placed into different hierarchical structures.

We become depressed because we did not get something we wished for or we did not experience what we wanted. We got hurt along the way, and the pain we experienced never left us. After time, this pain becomes something that is simply normal in our lives. I firmly believe that depression is a condition experienced when one neglects to accept the tragedies in their life as being beneficial to experience as a means of progressing in the future.

I tried for so long to comprehend the nature of depression, for it is something I, as well as many other people close to me, have experienced. Extensive thinking and pondering led me to believe that severe depression is as close to a hell—philosophically speaking—that we will ever experience in this life. Whether you believe that hell is a real place or not is beside the point. The idea is that this motif of hell could be most plainly shown to us through the debilitating characteristics of depression. And perhaps that is all we can ever do, because it is so complex we can only understand it through comparison to something that we know to be bad and of evil design.

Being honest and straight to the point with someone who is severely depressed is often a good way to lean. Sugarcoating the issue at hand will only give the individual a false sense of hope, and consequently, the individual will plunge into the darkest of depths that they could not fathom before. Truth liberates us. It will always be the hardest thing to hear, but it will always be the most necessary. Meaning in life is derived from truth, a full awareness of the world around that is shown through an unbiased viewpoint. Happiness, as well as all other beneficial emotions, can become lasting through meaning. I guess that leads us to the idea of what constitutes the definition of beneficial emotions, and to this I say, all emotions are beneficial, because even those that affect us negatively at first will subside in the end and allow us to learn.

I do believe it is good to experience depression, albeit modestly, simply because only then will we understand the distinct parameters that allow us to become depressed. Submit yourself to the greatest evil that you can possibly experience in life and see where that takes you. Submit yourself to the greatest virtue that you can possibly experience in life and see where that takes you. These ideas are entirely telling of an individual, and only along these parameters can we truly understand which way we inherently lean because of the societal structures we have established. Most of us would not want to lean toward the path of malevolence, although it seems that there are some people throughout history who have taken the malevolence out of all others and embodied it within themselves to carry out the greatest misdeeds we can think of. Most of the time, these individuals come from a past of unchecked depression, where nobody was present to lend a helping hand. That is why I genuinely advocate reaching out a hand to those around you that are suffering immensely. Be willing to help people deal with their issues, and only allow their issues to become a part of you if they are not fully dependent on your existence. As humans, we must be able to act upon instinct. Nobody should ever become our source of dependability, for we should often be able to help ourselves out when we are against the ropes. Obviously, we do not live in a perfect world, so you should truly praise those who are willing to sacrifice their day to help. I believe it is only through good deeds and charitable acts that we will ever see depression and other forms of mental illness decrease.

Mental illness is an area of high concern to me. Speaking from experience, I have seen mental illnesses such as schizophrenia, bipolar disorder, and anxiety wreak havoc on the lives of those close to me. Being young and coming from a background that has little to do with a clinical understanding of mental illness, I cannot provide much insight on the topic. That said, I do not believe mental illness is something addressed enough in schools and social settings for young adults and teenagers.

In the social-media age, we are beginning to see strong correlations between technology use and depression, primarily in teenagers. When a post is liked, commented on, etc., we are given a dopamine rush, similar to that experienced when drinking and having sexual intercourse. Those who develop an addiction to this dopamine response via social media stimuli are prone to be increasingly depressed, resulting from constant disappointment. For society to turn away from youth struggling with such an addiction is reprehensible. How can a society that firmly believes in advocating the importance of teenage sobriety not do the same with spreading awareness for social media–based depression? Time and time again, society will disappoint us, but it is up to the generation of today to claim the world of the future and bring about reform.

It has often disturbed me how often I hear of young boys being given medications for ADHD for simply demonstrating male personalities traits at a young age. Seeing as how diagnoses for ADHD became much more prevalent in the 1990s, it is worrisome when also researching the rising occurrences of mass shootings. Simply put, the prepubescent teenager cannot be subject to a high amount of chemicals at a young age, and I believe it is absolutely reprehensible that such a phenomenon is occurring without any reformation. At any rate, there is something to be said about how social settings may worsen the severity of mental illnesses or the way individuals with mental illnesses act, and rightfully so.

This brings us into the territory of discovering the ideals of cliques. The presence of the bully is something that is inherent in nearly all forms of societal apparatus, and in many ways, it is what defines certain defense mechanisms in the human psyche, including fear conditioning and persistent-type qualities. Given the situation that we subject an individual of psychological inadequacy into a destructive peer-group in the form of bullying—embodying harassment and greater forms of abuse—the effects can be cataclysmic. Such events are seen time and time again, although we continually do nothing, and it is reprehensible that it is allowed to go on. Perhaps I don't know how we fix this, and maybe there is no way to fix it, although progress does not always need an exact answer; many paths can be taken to discuss mental illness and bullying in schools. It is only when the school takes responsibility for being inadequate, as well as when students become advocates for the issue at hand, that we will see a lasting change.

The conclusion that the world is a manifestation of evil tendencies is a result of the selfish nature of society. There are far fewer philanthropists and social workers than greed-stricken profiteers of the suffering of the weak. And it is no wonder that people become depressed. All the trials people face, through all the suffering—partly imposed by the evil acts of others—only to lead to a sudden and terrible death. Although it should not be at the other end of the cycle wherein there is always safety, for the notion of safety provides a false sense of security, because we cannot grow when we are continually held back. It is necessary to experience forms of depression in modesty because it is best to be of a slightly vulnerable design, wherein there is always room for improvement to take place. When in this dimension of vulnerability, we are able to venture out and find out what it is that agonizes us, why it agonizes us, and furthermore, where we can avoid the suffering-based agony. In this region, it may be evident that suffering is at the pinnacle of understanding.

Depression should be seen as one of the many multitudes of dimensional sufferings that are experienced in life, and thus, it should be comprehended as a necessary obstacle to face, in cooperation with all the ramifications that it imposes on existence. Rather than succumbing to all of the negative self-thoughts that are inherently correlated with life, I believe we should use these thoughts as justification to do things we never conceived as part of our latter reality. It is important to use our inadequacies to push us forward.

Chapter 6

Meaning and Purpose

WHY LIVE? IT WOULD BE SO MUCH EASIER not to have come into existence at all. We are beings full of energy, made up of molecules that would be much more commonly found on their own than bonded together to form one big mass of flesh and bone. The absence of everything in the world would be much easier, and perhaps such an idea is easier to comprehend. Nihilists pride themselves on these ideas—that there really is no meaning to anything, that everything "just is." The appeal to being a nihilist—the idea that life is without meaning—is that you have no comprehension of suffering, for suffering is a result of faith in a value structure being doomed into submission. There is no way to disappoint a nihilist because they have no reason to live, for they are broken spirits. It is fine if you wish to follow this path, and I advise that you should search this world for your own beliefs, although I do believe that there has to be some explanation for complex human emotions, such as happiness, love, sadness, envy, and jealousy. It has been too often seen that individuals lean toward nihilism without having any comprehension of having done so. Social media has been one of the main contributors to this phenomenon, as people continually hold the idea that the world is out to get them. It is extremely difficult to explain structural bodies and the tendencies of man without there being any greater meaning. This is largely why I advocate meaning. It does not matter where you believe we derive our existence from, but it does matter that you generate a purpose, a basis upon which you direct your life.

I have endlessly pondered how it could be possible, in a world where a transcendent deity exists, that so many people, having done nothing wrong, are faced with great tragedy and suffering. I hated the idea that people had to be subjected to the conditions of embodied evil even when they were of the highest virtue. Through much of the reading I did during my research, I found that it is often more attractive for writers, particularly of the realist-fiction genre, to write about just individuals being subjected to all of the worst brutalities of life. Reasoning will lead you to conclude that this is because it is the one truth in life we are all shielded from. For example, nobody wants to discuss the process by which an innocent child is subjected to vile harassment and bullying and ends up committing suicide. But why? For we have been conditioned through false indoctrinations that our suffering should not be discussed in the mainstream. We have strayed so far as to entirely sell out to authoritarian groups, to the point where we are afraid to discuss the issues that differentiate us from the masses of people. Tragedy can look the exact same in two different people's lives, although suffering is an entirely different issue, unfolding in different ways among the lives of many.

Suffering is so complex, it is hard to grasp onto one such idea. I have no justification as to why, in a morally based world, such events could occur. After much research and applied thought of my own, I have concluded that suffering is a necessary evil that keeps order in the world. The only way to eradicate suffering would be to take away the application of free will imposed by man on society.

Free will is the basis of being. Given the situation that we take away the ability for individuals to act on their moral motives, we would submerge into a state of being either unequivocally peaceful or entirely malevolent; there would be no in-between in such a utopian/dystopian society. As beings of instinct, we must act on the choices that best suit how we are going to satisfy our value structure.

Previously, I discussed the importance of understanding all of the negative things that happen to us. Once we accept all the negative things, we are able to live hopefully in the manner that we desire. Obviously, there is no right way to live, but there are ways that may be beneficial to the wellbeing of your existence if you direct your life toward them.

Thinking on the aspect of living one's life to the fullest, I would advocate that you do what aligns with your identity. Never submit to the values of anybody else but you, with the exception of a legislative body. It is too often seen that people conform to ideas, and the only reason they do so is that the social apparatus they have subjected themselves to has created values based on their group identity. It is dangerous to identify fully with groups. We have seen this with radicals of all different political affiliations who are so enticed by one way of thinking that they neglect the entire basis of being, which is the impulse to act on individual belief.

Earlier in the book, I discussed the importance of discovering and understanding your identity to guide yourself along the path of life. After having done so, you may likely come to an area of conflict, where one is in a stalemate, lacking an understanding of which path to take. At this point, your best bet would be to ask yourself the question, "What will be most beneficial to my aspirations while also satisfying the value structure I have created?" Acting on your ambitions is the most important thing to do when finding a path in life; otherwise, you are simply wasting time. Time is the one constant in the world; everybody has the same amount of time in the day. For this reason, the excuse "I do not have enough time" should not be valid on any occasion.

Build your life around what matters most to you. Life is worth living when we happily engage in things that are beneficial to us. Having a structure of being based on our identity will benefit our lives more than we thought. The things that matter most to us are often very clichéd things such as family, friends, and our hobbies, although we do not have to limit it to such a degree. I do think it is almost better to build our life around the feelings, the values, and the characteristics of things that matter most to us rather than the things themselves. For instance, prioritizing love will keep us close to family and friends. Similarly, hobbies can be embodied through the priority to keep order, by means of our focus on what we desire.

It is often seen that people end up following a path that is less advantageous to themselves because they have not properly structured their life around what is inherently important. The things that are important to us are often easy to see, but we constantly overlook them in fear of not being accepted by other people. So I say, to hell with the other people; you must strive to be your own!

All things can be made sense of in life by means of finding a purpose, a reason that all is as it should be, and that through our conviction we will obtain what is needed. Purpose can be found through religion, ambition, love, etc. There are no exact means of finding purpose, for it is different among all people. Although purpose is something, even if we are unaware of it at the time being, that guides us through all of the actions that we come across. I believe that even the greatest atrocities of life can be neglected or counteracted by means of having an understanding of our purpose in this world.

Never listen to the masses of people, primarily the older generations, who have so long held the indoctrination that we must focus our lives around one such meaning. Purpose can be found in all things if it pertains to us. The purpose to help others, to act in a godly manner, to fight for what we believe in, to aspire for something greater—these are only a few such interpretations of the idea, which is open-ended to your mind. Find what guides you through trial and error. Comprehension of why we fall short in life is found through purpose, for all things can be justified if there is one supreme meaning in life that keeps all within the constraints of order.

Human beings, although superior to other creatures in many aspects, are not advanced enough to live a totally free life. If life consisted 100 percent of freedom, we would be dumbfounded, lacking any parameters to guide us. We would not know what is right or wrong. The order that confines us is necessary, or else all would potentially be doomed to ruin. Having a purpose gives us a guideline of what we must orient our lives around, due to purpose being something that is often inherent to our identity.

Through my own experience, I have been able to

entirely counteract the suffering that I endured in life by having a purpose. Among many other things, two of the main purposes I use to guide me in my life are God and the power of love, both of which have led me to find meaning in life. The year 2018 was terrible for me, consisting of family hardships, depression, and the loss of a great friend of mine. The only way that I was able to stick through and continue on with my passions in life was to accept God and love as the meaning for why life is worth living. As backward as it may sound, I had never been quite as happy in my life until after all these tragedies unfolded, for a grand idea struck me at the end. I realized that the reason why I enjoyed life so much, the reason why I loved existing in the world, was that life, in its simplest definition, constitutes in failure by means of death. Fantasizing over the idea of enjoying hardship, I wanted to contribute something of value into the lives of those experiencing immense suffering. After much thinking, I concluded that life—as we have known it to be for centuries—is the connection between moral virtue and evil, by means of an inverse relationship. Organized religion and faith in the principles of being would be unequivocally different, or rather nonexistent, given the chance that tragedy-based suffering did not exist.

All is at it should be in the world, and this is only further reinforced by comprehension of meaning. All the suffering faced, all the tragedies imposed upon the undeserving, all of the corruption inherent within those of power, is meant to be the way that it is, and we must accept this fact. It is only when we come to this realization that we can change anything and live life in the manner that we wish.

Chapter 7

Loneliness and the Crowd

I NEVER COULD COMPREHEND WHY PEO-
ple so strongly fear to be alone. There is an element to
solitude that I believe is beneficial to the existence of
rational thought in the mind of an individual. It goes
without saying that when we are alone, we are most susceptible to evil temptations of thought, primarily that
which is closely associated with depression. However,
the ability to endure evil thoughts without allowing
them to manifest is the ultimate test of the will of man.

Loneliness, in a modest amount, can be used as a
vital means of making sense of the world as it occurs. I
have always believed that loneliness is something that
can be experienced even in the presence of many; I have
never thought of loneliness as being determined as how
many people surround you at any given point in time.
The beauty of such an idea is that when holding this
conviction, where not a single person can change the

importance of self-thought, one can live independently of the rest of the world. Those who are entirely comfortable in loneliness—a realm where depression is knocking at one's doorstep—are mentally ready for whatever condition of fear is presented in one's life. Subjecting oneself to the closest embodiment of psychological hell while using it to their advantage prepares an individual for whatever terrible manifestation of chaos one must endure.

When alone, one must learn how to dedicate their time to the passionate aim of thinking about the problems that are going to make the world a different place. A wasted day occurs when the time is not taken to think about how the world could be changed. When you are alone, take time to examine the world around you. Ask yourself, "What inadequacies do people contain that can be fixed?" Search for problems. Understand everything. The world is incredible, and even the smartest minds will not be able to perfect the field of study they are in within their lifetime. High school kids must learn to recognize that the assignments they are given are simply a means of showing work ethic. The true work that should be done in youth should be learned through self-thought and discovery. Contemplating all the possible scenarios of how an event unfolds, of how people end up experiencing events, will help the individual transcend the limits that they previously recognized as parameters that confined them.

Those who associate with the complex structure of

the crowd are nothing more than the will of the group, which is simply a derivative of whatever a hierarchy leader believes. Never forget that the knowledge of one may be poison to the mind of another. The crowd never was. It has always been the individual who sits at the top of the social hierarchy, the alpha in a wolf pack. The wolf fails to act without the cohesive element of the group, but the bear functions as one unit, capable of complex individual strategy. The owl, capable of great wisdom, knows where to strike at a moment's notice and understands when to let prey live for another day. Although there is great strength in numbers, animal hierarchies show us the strength in individualism and wisdom. The crowd does not act on individual wisdom but on the wisdom of a figurehead, who neglects his subjects and, like a tyrant, silences their voices.

Those in power are in no position to decide what must be pitied, what must be hated, what must be valued. The individual and only the individual comprehends the complex structure of being. A group will never be able to tell you what you feel. They will never tell you, "I have suffered just the same as you have," for no suffering is found in the same form in more than one individual. Our minds are an embodiment of the butterfly effect, wherein any subtle change, had it occurred, would have caused us to think differently.

The individual is the embodiment of the thinking of every crowd that he has ever been in the presence of. It is only the combined knowledge of the leaders of groups, not the group members, that will harbor itself in the mind of the individual. The individual shows great displeasure in the crowd, for the crowd has become too powerful—from the will of the masses—to keep under control. Group ideology leads to collective suffering, and the individual knows this. He understands the tendency.

Those who identify with the pleasure of the crowd and pride themselves on the image that the crowd portrays of them are nothing when they are alone. When crowd-seekers are alone, they end up killing themselves psychologically, and in some tragic instances, physically. The individual, having been comfortable in solitude, goes on to lead the crowd. He does not lead the crowd for recognition, for he knows the tendency of power-seekers to become tyrants; he leads the crowd for the good of the individuals in the crowd so that they can go on to manifest greatness for themselves.

In any great group that has been an embodiment of good nature, it is a result of the leaders having based their mind on the principles of individual thought. Everything the group has, the group must contribute to the work of the individuals at the head. Individuals working together and a group of people working together are entirely different substrates. Individuality creates innovation, while the group simply elaborates on what the individuals thought up. Jobs and Wozniak founded Apple through efforts based on how two individuals believed they could change the world. The assembly workers put the computers together, and they play a pivotal role in the process, but the process was created by the individuals—those who took the time to think in their solitude about how the world could be different and how efforts could be minimized for the masses. This is the great power of loneliness: taking individuals into a state that is potentially dangerous, allowing them to think in a manner that spikes inquiry to create a new and better world. All great innovations came from an idea manifested in the mind of the individual, if not multiple individuals together.

To make yourself the strongest individual possible, you must have the mindset that you are the greatest asset available to any situation there is, granted that the objective is to fix the issue at hand. In all likelihood, you are not the person that is most qualified for any position in the workplace or for solving a problem of any other design, but you must adopt the mindset that you are infallible. You would be underrepresenting your talents if you based your mindset on courses of action that you have already experienced. Do not be afraid that you are inexperienced, for you will always be inexperienced in more than one aspect. None of us will ever reach what we portray in our minds as being the way to act. We have mindsets that are imperfectly manifested, and the beauty in such a thing is that we always have something to aspire toward. Perfection can only be reached by the transcendent, not the individual man.

Perhaps looking at stories of creation, regardless

of belief, is what gives us the best understanding of how vital individualism is to the life of man. If God constructed the world by himself, for the benefits of his people, then perhaps it is proven in such a case that the will of the individual is the strongest force to be reckoned with.

Politicians are hungry for the impressionable minds of Generation Z. Not being fully mindful of how the world truly works, the occasionally infantile minds of those within Gen Z can be lured into a political machine by means of a few kind words. We must not allow this to continue. We must not allow this targeting to stand. Gen Z is powerful beyond the recognition that is given to us

Never be fooled by the attractiveness of the crowd. The crowd will wish to entice you, own you, and take credit for the accomplishments that you earned by your-self. The most "toxic" of people belong to the crowd. Identity politics have only led to the heightening irra-tional behavior of crowd-based ideologies. In a time of intense political intervention in the lives of those who are easily tempted by the malevolent makeup of radical ideologies, I urge you to act on your own will and desire as an individual apart from the crowd. And thus I say to you, do not be the crowd; create the crowd.

Chapter 8

The Most Debilitating Disease: Fear

LURKING ON THE WEAK OF MIND AND body, it feeds, waiting for the death. The monster wants to overtake what belongs to him. Through the indecisive hesitations of man, the occurrences of saying "I can't" and "I am not good enough," he becomes most powerful. With his strength and power over the weak, he recites in their minds, "Call me by my name. Submit yourself to me, for I am Fear."

Fear is the fly who, upon landing on the meat, is enthralled with the idea that his eggs will produce hundreds of maggots that will decompose what was once a glorious creature. Fear is Satan taking pride in the workings of his processes to kill an individual, subjugating into a confined box of hellacious design.

Fear is inescapable. Most people who do not want

to be crippled by their fears simply resist them, but I tell you, resisting them is not enough; you must take ownership of what it is that made you afraid in the first place. The evil nature of the world wants you to resist your fears so that you can slowly deteriorate to the point of psychological ruin.

I never understood why people went on with their lives knowing very well that they had not handled their fears the way that they should have. Many people die pushing off the idea of fighting their fears head-on because they are afraid of losing something in the process. The only way to properly eradicate fear is to enter the void and climb out. There is no way to deal with the problems of the world without being willing to lose something in the process. If you are not willing to risk everything that matters to you to gain a better level of existence, then you are living a life without purpose. Fear must be finely understood because most of the time it is found in occurrences of when there is a risk of losing something that one values. For instance, an entrepreneur might fear putting his life savings into his startup because he believes that if the company fails, he will lose all of his assets. In many ways, I do not believe life is worth living without fears. Every great leap of faith came into existence because of the fear that an individual faced when in crisis.

It would be easy to say the world is not that complicated because people are too afraid to put themselves into the void of discovery to come out more knowledgeable in the end, even if they might damage themselves in the process. However, for those who have taken the risk, who have taken the leap of faith, they come out on the other side with a full understanding that the world is more complicated than they ever thought possible. They see that the world is way more complicated than the Bible says it is, than their education told them it was, or than any other false indoctrinations told them it was. People fear that learning anything other than what has been taught to them will leave them in a state of existential ruin, where all belief systems have been dismantled. I believe that the one thing keeping people from becoming successful is the fear that they will get hurt in the process of developing enlightened thinking. The resulting condition that is experienced after fear has been properly dealt with is enlightenment, for one has learned that one's fears are not defining forces in one's life, and they can be broken, dismantled, and killed themselves. Fear is a creation of man; just as a man can be killed, fear can as well.

Fear must be dealt with properly, for if it is not, it can entirely alter the direction that one's life should go. To every ambition, there is a fear waiting on the other side. This is a logical interpretation of the desire that is inherent with the human need to change. Either we allow things to change because we do not allow fear to override our ambitions, or we allow fear to break our ambitions in a way where we never even pursue them. Life is incredibly hard, and one of the reasons is that humans always second guess themselves, for they are not infallible, as their transcendent Father is. Humans do not understand the right course of action to take until they have been taught the correct manner to do so.

Because every human being is intrinsically different from the rest, the magnitude of fears varies for every individual. However, the proper way of dealing with the fears that one faces remains absolute across all dimensions. The most beautiful thing about life is that one is able to defeat the fears that one had thought of as inescapable while going on to endeavors thought to be impossible. Our fears limit our conceptualization of what is possible for us. In that sense, it would be best to act on our fears in the most proper manner so that we can understand exactly how capable we are of things we never thought possible.

I believe that human beings are destined for greatness from the point they enter the world. You cannot simply enter a world somewhere in between virtue and malevolence, destined to fail, without the ability to achieve something of greater importance. For why would there be life if not to manifest something of desire; there has to be a reason for it all. The only thing stopping human beings from achieving wonderful things are the fears associated with ambition. The tradeoff for possessing a higher intellectual capability than many other creatures is that we contrive ideas in our head based on past experiences and the shortcomings of others to interpret a destiny that would only be adequate in scale to what we can become. Knowledge is useful, although it must be used in the right ways to hold any value. Never allow your knowledge of prior events stop you from doing something that you genuinely believe is destined to happen.

The visionaries of the world allow their ideas to flow freely without the interaction of fears getting in the way. Seeing what your life can become is a valuable asset to ensure that one's time on this earth is spent properly. Although it is true that many of the things that we work hard at will be of no avail, the beauty in life is found through the ideas of the fall and the rise; when one door gets closed, build yourself back up again and direct your life toward another area that you are passionate about. If the conviction was held that you were going to be a success in one area, then your ability to believe will transcend all possible difficulties on the road to success. The moment will come when you obtain what you have desired, but only if you accept your fears, learn the tendencies that they hold, and act on them in a manner that will associate you with the best version of yourself.

The intrinsic qualities of fear can be manipulated so that they will be defeated or become a mere triviality. The characteristics embedded within life that are meant to bring about suffering shall not become limiting factors if you seek to preserve conviction over all others.

Chapter 9

Virtue and Evil

THE COMPREHENSION OF MORALS, whether in the life of a believer or in the life of an atheist, is what ensures that behavioral standards are met to keep life meaningful. Atheists and believers alike understand that not much differentiates the path of righteousness from the path of malevolence. That said, the two groups have different definitions of what constitutes moral right and wrong. Having discussed the dangers associated with group collective identities, I advocate, regardless of belief or lack thereof, that one be able to interpret right and wrong through one's own parameters.

Virtue in the eyes of one may be seen as pity in the eyes of another. The interpretation of evil through one's point of view may be an act of sacrificial virtue in another. Having a full understanding of the simplistic nature of morals and their inadequacies will allow one to act based on a rational interpretation of virtuous and malevolent behavior.

The Christian insists that his path is the only path to a life of fulfillment. He hides the disgust that he feels deep down for the atheist, which is a contradiction of the mannerisms of his savior Jesus Christ. The love he feels for his atheist neighbor is only shown because of pity; for he feels that his atheist brother may not be able to enter the kingdom of heaven. Only upon coming to the realization that God loves all people will he understand that God will allow the virtuous atheist to enter the kingdom of heaven.

The atheist insists that the Christian is a creature of dim-witted absurdity. He holds the conviction that churchgoers go to church only because they need the church, and he is right in this conviction, although he persecutes those who are in need of security. How could he live with himself knowing that he is persecuting those who need assistance, love, and compassion?

It is only through the cooperation of different belief systems that society will be able to function at a level of near utopianism. However, wishful thinking as such is ill-minded because it may bring about more harm than good. For if everybody acted as their most virtuous self, then there could be no differentiation among individuals, and we will have combined to form one brainwashed collective identity.

We see the importance of morality throughout the structure of the governing bodies of which we are citizens. Had we no legislature, had we no faith or moral foundation, it would all be meaningless—a society based on nihilistic anarchy. There would be no way to justify whether murder was wrong. There would be no reason to believe that humans should exist at the top of the dominance hierarchy. Without belief in anything, for all we know, brutish pigs could rule over all of us. In such a society, everyone would act based on one's own rationale. If they wished to rape, they would. If they wished to rob, they would be thieves. If they wanted to be cannibals, they would tear the flesh off of their neighbor's body. People need morals to guide them, or else there would be no way to control the self-inflicted hardships that humans would impose. In this sense, there is a meaning to everything. Whether the meaning behind the moral foundation is God depends on your own belief system, but our society has been founded on a sense of moral legislature and faith, and there is no way of attempting to discredit this argument; it is inherent in our identities.

One must create parameters that they define as virtue and evil and direct their life accordingly. Aim to be of the highest virtue, but accept that you will do things that are evil. There is not much that differentiates a man of virtue from a man who identifies with evil. It is often the case that the corruption of man is seen as a result of environmental conditions. Such is the case with Hitler and the Columbine shooters. In no sense should there be a justification for their actions, for they committed acts that are utterly abhorrent, although it must be understood that men are not born as leaders of genocide and as school shooters. These actions are taught, and conclusions are often drawn under the most severe occurrences of human suffering that lead people down this path.

Examining the qualities that characterize the evil men of history is important to understand that not much differentiates you from one who walks the path of evil, besides a few small life choices. I would recommend pondering how such men could have committed the atrocities that they acted out, for this thinking will hopefully direct you to the path of virtue.

Have sympathy and a heart full of love for every individual you come across because you will never understand the complex internal conflicts they may be experiencing. Although strong on the outside, the human being is susceptible to weakness on the inside. People struggle immensely over trivial matters because they have not built their life on a proper foundation. Create your foundation upon your concept of good and evil, and you will find contentment in your own heart.

I have found that humbleness is one of the most proper signifiers of a just individual. Staying humble will leave no doubt in the minds of others that you are a higher caliber person. In success, be proud and remember all of the tribulations you faced on the road to get to where you are, but celebrate only inwardly. In defeat, acknowledge your faults and move on. Casting out this image for all to see will give others a sense of how a virtuous person should act.

The impressionable minds of teenagers are subject to resorting to rash decision-making, primarily because it is easy to coax individuals who experience angst and long for affection. We see universities and even some high schools that attempt to mold the minds of naive students into accepting their ideologies which the professor holds to be of indefinite truth. Before I mentioned the importance of neglecting what "the professor" says. The only reason for saying this is that I believe—through the introduction of common core—a manifold of issues has come about, including the desire for teachers to create ideologues rather than knowledgeable students. Students must search for their own truth. Among the many impressionable students that I attended high school with, teachers were able to change their views just by sounding competent and sincere. Because teenagers live in a world of constant suffering, they will listen to anybody who treats them with respect, for they may not feel safe in any setting other than the classroom. I am immensely grateful for the teachers who introduced their political ideologies into a classroom setting because I was able to search for my own truth in a time where I was going through an existential crisis. For many, however, I know this is not the case, because they were fooled by the soft-spoken words that seemed to be helpful. I believe this is utterly reprehensible and shows how even when an event may be looked at as a decree of virtue, when observed through a finer glass, it turns out to be based upon evil intentions—the intention to transform minds of immense pain, agony, and distrust, promising them an ideology that will help them now only to abandon them years later.

Learn to pick out the evil intentions that exist in the virtuous actions of those who wish to help others. For it is one of the great flaws of life: because man is largely fallible, when he wishes to act in a just manner, there remain underlying intentions that exist only because there is some benefit for him. The will to benefit is perhaps the only truth that is absolute, for all things are done for the benefit of some individual. Even the most selfless individual does things because he feels content after helping others. If we hold virtue and evil on separate ends of the spectrum of morals, then wherein lies the will to benefit?

We must act on the value structures that have been created and carried out for centuries, for if we neglect the shared values that make our existence of some greater importance, then we will have subjected ourselves to a life where all hope is lost. Moral systems are the only things that keep human beings thinking rationally. Morals give people a reason to live. Perhaps the will to benefit is the most important aspect of the system itself; it is a dichotomy that depends on intention. For the will to benefit may bring about contentment in one who risks his life for his neighbor, although it may also be seen when one has killed his neighbor to steal his wealth.

We cannot come to a unanimous consensus of what constitutes good and evil. The minds of immense virtue and the others of wretched wickedness would skew apart the definitions of the distributions to the point where it is entirely polarized. In this sense, the only true definition of moral behavior can be constituted through the interpretation of the individual. The strength of the enlightened individual over the blinded group is incalculable, and the relevance of this idea is not understood by the younger generation. It pains me deeply to see how blindly people walk down paths simply because they have been cleared to do so by the crowd. Only the individual, with indefinite moral understanding that has led him in the direction of truth, will be able to live a contented life. The individual does not have to fear that he has to be morally perfect, for truth has shown him that, due to his flaws, he can never obtain this type of perfection. Henceforth, the individual walks with his purpose in his right pocket and his happiness within the spindle on his back.

> And now that you don't have to be perfect, you can be good.
> —John Steinbeck, *East of Eden*

Chapter 10

Want vs. Need

DESIRE IS A FALSE PERCEPTION OF WHAT is needed in life. This idea is elementary, although it holds a great amount of validity, for even the simplest truths are still true. It is beneficial to do some things based on the justification that you simply wanted to do them, although it could be very detrimental to your wellbeing if your life becomes a manifestation of all that is wanted. Necessity holds even greater value in every sense conceivable. It is entirely basic to the idea of success that all things beneficial derive from what is needed. Look at your own success compared to the economic idea of supply and demand. If your life demands a higher amount of output, you must supply it with a greater amount of things that must happen, not the things that will make life expedient.

For those of whom come from a broken past, make sure to engage in situations that you need to engage in.

It is of no help to your future self if you avoid the things you need to do simply because you are too hesitant or afraid. You cannot control your fears, and they must not dictate the things that you do in your life. A drug addict fears becoming sober and enduring months of rehab, but he does it anyway because he knows that it will be beneficial to him in the end. When we can make the things that we want into the things we need, we will be able to live at a higher standard than where we previously stood.

Although life is intrinsically complex even in its most basic dimensions, what we need can be easily found just by pondering the different aspects of our life. Possible questions, targeted primarily at individuals that struggle immensely, may look like the following:

1. Where am I prone to being inadequate?
2. What is it that I commonly identify with?
3. What addictions overtake me?
4. Do I associate closer with the moral or immoral side to myself?

The beauty in the answers to the questions at hand is that they cannot be embodied in a single answer. The questions are broad in scope, and they are that way for a reason. Only when you can interpret your problems on a large scale will you ever be able to tackle the heart of the issue at a micro-scale.

Being individuals that wish to identify only with

the actions we want to identify with, we must partially untrain our minds to counteract the feelings of want in order to target the things that we need. We are responsible for doing the things we need to do. It is dangerous to cast ourselves blindly out into the world with a false sense of what is important. In a deeper sense, what is important is usually what is a basic need for us.

Do not continue to womanize if you need love. Dear friend, I promise you that the repercussions of denying the love you have for a significant other are defeating your purpose in this world. If there is a girl you know you love but have forgotten for your own convenience and sexual desires, go back to her. That girl is the one who you need to keep yourself in a state of contentment and appeasement.

I urge you to get up from your parents' sofa, stop getting high all day, and find a means to live that will benefit you. Understand the pain you impose on your parents while they are at work and you sit on the couch all day getting stoned. My friend, I promise you that the habit you have subjected yourself to will not benefit you years down the line. There is much more to life than the two-hour-long rush from the chemicals that you are injecting into your system. The passion for becoming successful, the love in doing what is needed to be done, is much more gratifying and freeing than the bottle of pills and the fifth of Jack Daniels in your hand.

To my defeated entrepreneur, I say to you, keep on pushing, for the time is not quite right for you. It feels

safe to harbor within a wall of self-pity when your idea
fails, but this is not the right course of action to take.
Utilize the time to go over your business model and
eradicate all possible flaws in the plan. If the market
was not right, then keep enduring failure until the market turns around. Be willing to go into a large amount
of debt if it means that a return on investment will
come about. You are responsible for turning yourself
around and becoming the success that your impover-
ished fourteen-year-old self believed you could be.

It will always feel safer doing the things we want to
do because they do not pose any inherent risk. You owe
it to yourself to become the success you once saw years
earlier. There is no shortcut to becoming successful;
you must act on every single thing that you are responsible for doing.

I have thought extensively on the effects of having a
want-based society vs. a need-based society. I came to
the hypothesis that some aspects would not be entirely
different from what we already see today. Although
every single individual has a different story, there are
tendencies within certain groups that are quite evident
without giving much thought into the idea itself. Most
of the people who identify with the things they want
and not the things they need will end up becoming more
prone to addiction, in every sense imaginable. Most
of the people who feel a sense of responsibility feel a
sense of moral obligation, wherein they desire to act out
the things they feel they must do. By these standards,

the two groups will polarize into two sections of success, largely distinguishable from each other. In the absence of success will be found the people who only ever did the things that they wanted to do, without doing the things they needed to do. On the other end of the spectrum are those who identify with acting in a manner that relates to an understanding of underwritten responsibility.

The inclination to do what is needed is the only means of creating any form of sustainability in life, in all applicable dimensions. Do not fall victim to the desires that make you feel safe, for they provide a false sense of security. Be comfortable submitting yourself to agony and pain if it means that the "you" you will become is better off than the "you" that you are now. Make it a habit to do the things that are needed to obtain success, and you will live a life full of contentment rather than a life full of needless suffering. My friend, I promise you that the world of tomorrow is much greater than the world of today, but it will only be that way if you are willing to sacrifice your desires for your responsibilities.

Chapter 11

False Indoctrinations

FROM OUR GENESIS, WE ARE TOLD TO BE-have in a way that is most convenient and beneficent for whoever is teaching us. If we say things that come from within, ideas based upon incredible honesty, we are sold short for being incredulous. This is part of the reason why it is so frowned upon when the generation of today tries to dismantle any idea that was introduced by prior generations. The influence of parents is one of the driving forces for the obtainment of knowledge and proper behavior, although parents themselves may get a great deal wrong. Many parents believe their author-ity, specifically the false justification that being older results in wisdom, is a reason to disregard whatever is said by their offspring. There is a lot that previous generations have gotten right, primarily the relevance of taking responsibility, although, depending on the belief of the parent, there is much room for reform of

false indoctrinations that the older generations hold
onto. I am in no way advocating becoming a rebellious
teenager, although I do believe one should be skeptical
whether what you are taught is certain to be true.

Human beings are creatures of bias, for it is within
our nature to do whatever is best for our survival. In the
same way, humans will do whatever is best to ensure
that what they teach others holds to be of absolute truth.
This is one of the great flaws of the habitual actions of
humans. Never be absolutely certain that you—or anybody else for that matter—is entirely correct.

Social media has allowed the current generation
to be seemingly all-knowing when it comes to events
taking place within pop culture. However, the tradeoff
of becoming technologically advanced is an inestimable
amount of incompetence as a result of believing what
the older generation claims. In all likelihood, CNN,
Buzzfeed, Vice, and Fox are publicizing ideas based
on what is most advantageous to the respective news
networks. Do not take me for an individual who hates
journalists, for I think it is an honorable profession,
although I do not believe journalists—or anybody, for
that matter—should be idolized as speakers of truth.

It would be wise for you to think as an individual and not to conform to the indoctrinations of the
past generations. This is part of why I so greatly fear
angst-ridden teenagers who associate themselves with
the collective identity of the two-party system. At a
young age, do not be so sure that the Democrats or the

Republicans speak of absolute truth, for the general nature of the two-party system is based on the appeal to the masses. Avoid believing in every single policy that a given party has to offer. I despise the idea of associating as a working unit within the monster of a political party, for you have no insight into whether the indoctrinations, purporting to be based on higher standards, are of any value whatsoever.

If an individual wishes to push their ideas on you, do not give them the attention they so greatly desire. All the group wishes is to gain another supporter who will become another foolish ideologue working within their machine. It is comfortable when one accepts the ideas of the group because it requires no effort whatsoever; effort is required to ponder ideas and fit them into one's perception of the world accordingly. Accept the truth that you will have to be uncomfortable to do anything worthwhile in life. There is a reason why we are not meant to share all the same ideas. God would not have created us if we thought with only one brain, for if everyone thought the same way, we would be as useless as if we had never come into existence at all.

Why do we not stress the importance of teaching the evils associated with communism? Such an answer is genuinely simple, although not many are willing to stick up to the tyranny of the education system, and the political climate for that matter, to tell them they are entirely wrong. The reason why we do not teach how communism is a corrupt system is that the crowd is too afraid to admit that equality of outcome is one of the greatest absurdities that has ever come into creation. Make sure to read my words clearly: do not confuse equality of opportunity with equality of outcome, as they are entirely different concepts. I am an advocate for equality of opportunity, although I believe that equality of outcome is one of the greatest embodiments of evil intention that we have seen since the time of communism. Equality of outcome, an idea that many are trying to entice the younger generation with, will lead to the extinction of the individual. Although I am not a conspiracist in the slightest sense, I do find it intriguing how society so strongly wishes to defeat individual identity.

Be sure to listen carefully to all that you are told, for you may come to a fallacious conclusion on the basis of not stressing the importance of awareness and understanding. The stray from the liberal and conservative beliefs has taken people to the collective identities of the despicable left and the detestable right, respectively. I pride myself on being genuinely explicit when rattling off the ideas I come across, so once again, be able to understand the difference between the party—which favors the individual due to its close proximity to the center of the political spectrum—and the group collective identities of the left/right. Both sides of radical group identities are equally reprehensible, although it is more frequently seen that the left intervenes in matters pertaining to destroying individual thought, specifically among the impressionable teenagers of this generation.

Due to the incompetence of the large majority of teen-agers, they hear the words "equality of outcome must be absolute," and they are sold on the idea without a second thought because they prioritized the word "equality" over the entire phrase, which gives the word two en-tirely different connotations.

Do not assume that simply because words such as justice, freedom, and equality are said in a phrase that the speaker must be saying something of relevance. The given words can have entirely different connotations in phrases such as "justice for murderers," "freedom for rapists," or "equality for all wages." These phrases are entirely contrived to put emphasis on the point at hand, but they do get across the idea nevertheless. If there is one thing I wish to accomplish through this book, it is to make teenagers more competent, so they can act on their own individual ideas and knowledge to piece together whether an idea is of value. I greatly fear the future of individual freedom if we continue to persecute the individual for acting on one's beliefs. The left cannot stand seeing the success of a strong-willed individual, so they impose labels such as "fascist" and "Nazi" to get the point across that the person they are persecuting is a threat to the sovereignty of the group identity. The weak-minded do not want to identify with anything other than the group identity, for they fear that if they do, they will become a "Nazi," just like the other individual, and as a result, the group gains another follower out of fear. All the group can ever impose on the individual is fear. Fear of persecution in the most vile and abhorrent form.

We must stray from the tendencies of this age, the indoctrination which holds that the individual is a threat to societal wellbeing. We are blessed knowing that we live in a society that prioritizes equality of opportunity, for it is the greatest advancement imposed on society in aid of the individual. Although we must not let this idea get brushed behind us, as is the case when people see it as unfair that an individual creates a towering enterprise, and all of a sudden, people hate equality of opportunity and wish for equality of outcome. It goes without saying that there will be some amount of inequality among all things, even within the safety net surrounding equality of opportunity.

There is a great power that exists in dismantling the prior notions that people must be sorted into groups. To be of an intent that is beneficial to the existence of the individual, throw yourself into the middle of the chaos, into the middle of the arguing ideologues, and piece together what is true and what is invalid. The ability of humans to create ideas and act on them is one of the greatest evolutionary adaptations in the animal kingdom. It is due to our superior intellect, in cooperation with our necessity to act on the will of the individual, that sets us at the top of the hierarchy of being.

We may look at warfare as one of the prime ex-amples of where the will of the individual exists, thus creating an accurate analogy for the premise of my argument. It is not the case that an army is simply a large grouping of men taught to carry out one task, for humans are much too fragile to act perfectly in accordance with the orders of the superior. Although the resulting product may be what a superior officer intended, the intent of the individual soldier carrying out the mission may be entirely different. Armies are collective bodies, but they are bodies comprised of many free-thinking individuals acting on their own will to benefit some party, whether this is an individual or a group.

It is a common misconception that groups that are non-ideology based act only on the demands of a superior or a leader. The order of the superior may be carried out, but it is only through immense scrutiny and moral pondering that the resulting action occurs. For example, had you not been taught that doing your chores was a necessary responsibility, you would have to think about the task at hand, acting upon the will to finally carry out what you were told.

Your best bet at living a life of omnipresent satisfaction is to allow yourself to think as we were meant to, as individuals. If there is no option except to identify with the group, as in the case of a politician or a businessman, surround yourself with people who think as individuals for the betterment of mankind as well as one's individual will. The only way to maintain the sovereignty of the individual is to question everything but to find a means upon which to identify.

Chapter 12

Surroundings

WHAT YOU SURROUND YOURSELF WITH IS contagious. Whether it be people, ideas, or even other physical objects, they all have a large impact on us, in various ways. Although I am quite fond of the idea of surrounding yourself mainly with what you identify most closely with, I do believe that there is much more in life than the comfort one feels when ensconced within a safety net. Life is experience—it truly is—and the more we enable ourselves to see all things and to feel all things, the greater benefit we will receive.

There is much to the world, and it is highly likely that the majority of us will never be able to see all the things that we wish to in our lifetime. That being the case, we should aim to experience and see as much as possible in the short life that we live. Although clichéd in the greatest sense, "you'll only live once," and the more we begin to act on this idea, the greater we will be able to help those around us, for we have experience in which they simply have no insight.

Picture in your mind all the things you want to see, all the people you want to meet, and hold the picture dear to you so you can ensure you have at least one driving force behind your existence. Do not conform to the idea that you are limited by money or other such material possessions, for if you wish to experience things, there are likely other ways to experience them, and if not in an exact way, you may be able to experience the same feelings of content in another manner, perhaps artificially.

The people you surround yourself with will often infect you with whatever characteristics they possess. In the case of a group of friends, it is likely that you will share the same interests, for that is partly what constitutes in the definition of a friend. However, you must be careful not to act only as a group but as a group based on free-thinking ideals. If you surround yourself with highly intelligent people, chances are you will benefit from any experiences—even arguments—you have with the given group.

Never be afraid to interact with those who are superior or inferior to you in any way. There is a lot that can be learned by examining the tendencies of individuals that have experienced varying levels of success. Talk to as many people in this world as you possibly can, for you never know if the stranger you introduce yourself to needs the kind of reassurance that will keep them from ending it all. Chances are you can help people deal with their issues just by discussing the issues they face and by advising them through your own rational thought. Humans face a lot of the same issues, and if we can simply talk to our neighbor and give them reassurance, perhaps we can make them see, after all, that life is meaningful and there is a lot of value in living a life of purposeful intent rather than waiting for death to take us.

In order to reach a level of success that is desirable, consider speaking to individuals who have experienced similar hardships to you, eventually going on to their own paths of success. Having a mentor in this world, other than a father or family member, can be of great use to someone wanting to hear advice from an unbiased point of view, wherein they tell their own version of the truth without a care for the feelings of those who are listening. It is these "hard truths" that must be understood to begin living a life that is unequivocally greater than the day prior. Making a large leap in success in a single day is distinctively rare, so you must aim to be a certain percentage—regardless of the degree of the percentage—better than the day before.

I never could grasp why people fear and exploit the homeless simply for being unshaven and unhygienic. There is a lot of knowledge that can be learned from homeless people if, God forbid, you actually sat down to talk to them about various aspects of life. Just as all human beings can tell you something that you may have been unaware of prior to a conversation, the same is true with anyone that holds a lesser economic standard than you. Treating the less fortunate as if they are some spectacle is wrong beyond recognition, and if you wish to bring about just action in the world, perhaps you should start by helping those that are at a lesser level of success than you. In no way am I advocating for creating a social safety net, but I am rather encouraging people to act with the goodness in their hearts, helping others without being obligated to do so.

The setting you immerse yourself into is nearly as important as the people you are surrounded by. Your location affects how you think, feel, and act to a large degree. In a world of constant industrialization and its negative side effects of pollution, it is often hard to seek the harbor of a blissful, stress-free environment. For this reason, your best bet may be to seek out nature as a means for spiritual appeasements between positive and negative forces.

I would advise you to seek some sort of affinity for nature, for the visions that one has when in the wilderness can be very thought-provoking and meditative. Sunsets, rainbows, and waterfalls are all creations that were meant to be seen by us, and depending upon our beliefs, symbolize something of much greater importance than we might have conceived. Just as there is great beauty in nature, there is a lot of necessary evils that one must visualize in order to keep their ego in check while also allowing for a way to experience a wide range of emotions. Seeing as how nature can be so magnificently beautiful yet so atrociously calamitous, one might assume humans are entirely the same. The events and objects that surround us are speaking to us, telling us things that we may know but whose significance we have forgotten. Upon visualizing phenomena in real life rather than through a computer screen, we will become genuinely better off, having the ability to draw connections between the physical world and our own convictions that we hold to be of some relevance, in regards to how the world ought to be.

The natural world can teach us a lot, especially as we witness how man imposes his will upon it. As an avid hunter, I accept the fact that the spirit of the kill is a necessary beauty. To me, hunting has always been a sacred and meaningful experience, for the taking of any creature's life is something to be done methodically and with care. Being alone in the fields, or in the blistering desert winds, great respect develops between man and nature, for nature will do its best to make sure man has to work for his desires.

Upon taking the life of an animal, the symbolic nature of being is understood through the organism, for it represents the fragility of life and the need for death. As terrible as it sounds, someone will always benefit from the death of another, perhaps even an individual halfway across the world. We are all interconnected, and the smallest of human phenomena can have a life-altering effect on an individual that we have never met. This idea exactly represents why we should always treat people with the goodness in our hearts, hoping to bring about a systematic pay-it-forward means of human righteousness.

The people surrounding us need us more than we can possibly conceive upon first glance. The problems within every individual surely vary, but there are ways of aiding those in need. Realize that even those who give the perception of a happy individual may be exceedingly far from being happy. A smile is never telling of one's inner thoughts, and that must never be forgotten. A prime example of this would be Robin Williams, a man who brought joy to many with his comical expressions and happy-go-lucky attitude but who dealt with severe symptoms of depression to the point of suicide (rest his soul). Depression is a hauntingly terrible thing, and it is one of the driving reasons why I want to see a change. I cannot bear to see people destroyed by their own minds any longer, and I believe that the more people who change their thinking, the better off we will be. We cannot continue to hold the same convictions of how we believe an individual's outward appearance reflects any internal conflict they possess, for this is only partially true in the rapidly moving and advanced society we live in. Surround yourself with people from as many various backgrounds as possible, in an attempt to help others work on behalf of a virtuous effort.

Besides the obvious physical surroundings that we must take notice of, our mental surroundings must be taken into consideration as well. The safety we find in our minds is without a doubt the most important aspect of living to our utmost potential. The ways we deal with adversity, suffering, and pain all affect our mental fortitude. Establishing a means to engage in a meditative state of being allows for rational-based thought. Having a clear mind is key in order to help those around you, to think critically, and to plan out a path to success.

Although I am a beginner in the realm of meditation, it has helped me deal with many issues, as it has helped many colleagues deal with theirs. The way in which I immerse myself into a meditative state is as follows:

1. Find a dark room.
2. Sit, lay, or monk-sit on a flat surface (i.e., floor).
3. Play neural stimulation music (not needed but helps a great deal; a vast collection is available on the Internet).
4. Breathe in for four counts, and exhale for four counts.

The preceding directions are simply suggestions and can be altered in a manner that best suits the given individual. The overall objective of meditation is to enter an abysmal state of mind, where the unconscious and conscious mind amalgamate, resulting in an enlightened, high-like experience. In this way, meditation is a viable alternative to substance abuse, just as many pursue running as a blissful stimulus during rehabilitation efforts.

Formatting your psychological setting in a way that is going to be most productive to efforts you are passionate about will allow for extrication of thought from the oppressive forces of fear and suffering. A clear mind is powerful. A man with the ability to control the force that imposes the most terror upon himself has nothing to be afraid of in the real world. Our minds are vastly complex and often perceive the severity of a situation to be much greater than it actually is. Our perception of an event as being fraught with danger is entirely telling of the nature of our mind and its own idiosyncratic tendencies. Fear is normal, and it dates back to our genesis, flowing through evolutionary psychology as we know it. However, if we deliberately create a present fear stimulus without there being a justifiable reason, we allow our minds to overpower us. This is why it is important to keep the mind in check through meditative efforts.

Our surroundings shape us. We cannot deny the power that is exerted upon us by the phenomena and people near us; whether it alters our emotions or our decision making, everything that we include ourselves within will have an effect on us. Look at human beings in relation to their surroundings as eggs during incubation; if they are not in the right climate and setting, the eggs will cease to exist. Everything that is around us shapes us into a version of ourselves that is different from the one that existed before.

Chapter 13

Awakenings

WHAT IF LIFE WERE OF A NATURE SUCH that it was simply a principle of reconstitution? Surely the Buddhists understood this idea, but perhaps they conceived it to be an idea entirely different from the foundation of being. In all likelihood, the idea I am proposing has little to no correlation with any idea of religion and more to do with philosophical inquiry.

We are taught that the law of conservation of energy is the principle that energy is neither created nor destroyed but rather reconstituted from one dimensional form to another. None of us thinks twice about this idea because it seems to be self-evident, and we are expected to believe the proposed concept. Accepting this fact, one can certainly conceptualize the idea of a spirit being reconstituted into another form. I mean, if an individual is alive, their spirit is wholly lively, and we proclaim that an individual is "full of energy." If one denies this, perhaps they have an entirely different definition of what it means to be alive.

For many, it is not clear what it means to be alive. Yes, if you have a pulse, that means that you are living, although maybe being alive is entirely different. We hear stories about people who, when nearing the end of their life, seem to be already dead, or at least they have convinced themselves to believe the idea that being bedridden in a hospital, while simultaneously being fed through a tube, defeats the purpose of living. We are taught that living is the ability to act on ambition, to be imaginative and create a world that we wish because of the will of our own conscious thought processes. I do believe that it is sometimes possible to predict an approaching death on the basis of listening to one's thoughts about how they are living and if they are doing it effectively. Our minds are powerful beyond human comprehension. How far beyond, exactly, will always be a mystery to us, although I firmly believe that the way one thinks can alter one's likelihood of living or dying. I have seen it many times over, particularly in the lives of family members close to me, that upon nearing death, their personalities degenerated into a state that was almost unidentifiable as being the loving human being I once knew. It is this degeneration of the human psyche where a fine line exists between being alive and dying. Keep in mind, I did not say the fine line between living and dying, and this was entirely intentional, because I believe that even when we are living there are aspects of us that are degenerating, and these same aspects are present only when we are "alive."

Having understood my definition of being alive, try to comprehend the idea that perhaps when we die, we awaken into a realm wherein it is not too entirely different from the realm we live in currently. Perhaps when we die, our comprehension of what the world around us should look like dies with us. If the same energy is attributed to thinking about the world is used in keeping us alive then perhaps, granted that the law of conservation of energy proves to be true, we are in a realm not entirely different than what we lived in before. If we believe in heaven, then it is quite likely that our spirit, as well as the energy associated with it, moves into this biblical heaven. The mind is all too powerful, and it is likely that the world we comprehend after death is simply an awakening of absolute wisdom within our spirits, wherein we finally understand that the secret to our existence is not entirely complicated but rather greatly conceivable.

Assuming that the former ideas that were intro-duced are relevant, it is not too farfetched to believe that we once again meet the people we are in contact with in the current realm in the spiritual post-living domain: heaven. In the beginning, we awaken into life, in life we live, and in the end, upon death, it is not that our spirit dissipates into nothingness, but rather, it transcends to another dimension, and though the dimension may be unknown to us at the time being, we know this is the case.

Technology has made it so that we have abandoned our belief systems at a staggering rate. Many of those who do not forthrightly state they are atheists are dealing with a battle within their own conscious mind, wherein they are generally afraid to go against their own intellect. In the intellectual world, it is frowned upon to promote any idea that seems to be irrational in nature. This is exactly why people turn from religion, for no aspect of religion is rational, because we have not seen visual evidence. However, the basis of faith is believing in something that is likely irrational at its core.

For scientists opposed to religion, they announce that perhaps a big bang is what created the universe. After pondering and hypothesis gets them to the point that they cannot get any further, the question comes into their mind: "Where did the energy needed for a bang to occur result from?"

Christians who denounce science believe that God is the answer to everything. After being able to back their argument upon the idea that "something cannot come from nothing," they eventually come to a crossroads wherein they have no explanation for the dinosaurs. The fact that science has led us to discover that the earth is 4.5 billion years old has strayed believers away from the Bible, for it is told that the earth was created and rested upon in the span of seven days.

It is only when we learn that a cooperative effort must be made that we can realize that God wanted us to discover the secrets of the universe. When this idea is spread to a vast degree, science and religion will be both equally respected. It is true that society cannot function without religion. An individual may be able to function without belief, but a society cannot, and there is absolutely no room to argue the case of the other side. It is also true that science must be used in order to describe how the cosmos came to be, and how beings such as ourselves came into existence.

Jung discussed the idea of death and rebirth as being a common motif associated with the archetype of the hero. When saying this, he hit it right on the nail. He truly had a niche for understanding the most complex aspects of humanity and simplifying them into ideas that could be comprehended by the masses. This idea is particularly true in the case of the adolescent, or an individual experiencing anxiety, angst, or some other form of existential crisis. When a teenager feels misunderstood or unimportant, they lose themselves (death), and if they are wise enough, they find themselves again (rebirth). For those who get lost without having found themselves again, the repercussions can be devastating: addiction (alcohol, drugs, sex, etc.), depression, and in very severe cases, suicide. Given that the wiser of the two paths is taken, the individual will awaken, hopefully finding themselves more mentally resilient than they were before. This goes down to the heart of the idea of awakenings symbolically tying in with human existence.

It is often the case that we will go through a man-ifold experience of awakenings in our life. Due to the idea at hand being capable of different interpretations in the life of various individuals, it is hard to say exactly how such a scenario may look. An addict going to re-hab and becoming sober, a man deserting womanizing and forming a lasting relationship, a prisoner leaving a penitentiary and going on to pursue a career—these are all prime examples of how one could "awaken" while living. Although, as we know the human race to be foolish, it is likely that one will awaken only to die and be reborn all over again.

Never be afraid to abandon the course of action you are pursuing if it means that you will learn something of great value. Learning is key to finding meaning, for the more that we learn, the more that we can get a grasp on what truth is and furthermore what our truth is. We will always have the opportunity to resort to the things we were working on before, but we will not always have the same opportunity to learn, especially if it is the case that an individual wishes to teach you something. Never take other peoples' time for granted. In all likelihood, when it is convenient for you to listen and learn from them, they will be dead. We will always find an excuse as to why it is not a convenient time to pursue something, but the more we focus on cutting out excuses, the greater people we will become, and we will become wiser for doing so. There will never be a convenient time to do something, so pursue it now rather than pushing it off to a later date.

Just as you should never postpone learning from somebody, you must also ensure you refrain from devoting energy to someone who devalues your time or opinion. Any allotment of time devoted to a non-reciprocating individual can be reallocated to the pursuit of knowledge, meaning, and success. I genuinely believe that the more knowledgeable we become, the more change we see in ourselves; we are constantly being reborn. Knowledge is key to understanding and adopting thought processes of our own, which will allow us to act on the ideas that we ponder over.

Do not be afraid to awaken from the rationality that you as well as the surrounding world have clouded over your conscious mind. Life is not always as it seems, and there is a vast amount of hidden meaning and reasoning that goes beyond the element of rational understanding.

Chapter 14

The Appeal to Knowledge

THERE ARE WAYS IN LIFE TO BECOME knowledgeable without having to follow the traditional path of education. Having a college degree with your name on it does not make you a more valuable asset to society than anyone else. That is not to say that college is useless, for if you take your time seriously, you can make beneficial use of the time dedicated to college. Never sell yourself into the belief that going to school is going to make you any better off than if you were to teach yourself, read, and make connections within the field of work you are wishing to pursue. Remember, school is in a large part about engaging within a different social setting than staying at home to learn.

Our abilities are much greater than we often perceive at first glance. For this reason, people often think that they cannot teach themselves as well as a teacher could. Teaching is an honorable profession, and I do believe there is substantial importance associated with the educating profession, although I believe academia as we know it is trying to push their agenda so much that they forget to teach students skills that will be beneficial when they are facing the post-schooling hell that is life. Although this issue is not nearly as lamentable as it is in the university setting, the issues are slowly creeping in as students feel safe within the ideas of "equity" and "freedom from the hurtful words of others."

I would advise you to seek to become an individual who is knowledgeable and wise enough to act on your decision-making in a way that is best suited for your own ambitions. A way to do this that is often swept under the rug in the twenty-first century is to read and take note of the ideas and the "whys?" behind every idea that is read. Literature is a domain for understanding and an aid to those who are in desperate need of a purpose. You do not have to be a "bookworm" in order to learn something of value from a book; it is obvious that books can be written about literally anything, so there is always an option out there that will suit your interests.

In the case of many authors, the books they write are an accumulation of all the wisdom and knowledge that they have accumulated throughout their life. Minds such as Nietzsche, Jung, Tolstoy, Dostoevsky, Steinbeck, Hemingway, etc., have all made vast contributions to the literary world, and their works contain a vast amount of insight into the mechanisms of being and the way that human beings interact in both their most glorious moments and in their follies. If you figure that most authors have done a great amount of research before writing their works, in some sense, when you read a work by one author, you may also indirectly pick up knowledge from the previous generation of authors. Processing the information, thoughts, and ideas of former generations will put you in the best possible position to act on your own will, deciphering how you need to live your life.

In correlation with literature, it is often wise to seek the advice and wise words of people with more authority than you in their respective fields of study. Social media, particularly YouTube, has allowed for the ideas of wise individuals to appear in your feed routinely, giving a constant means of gathering more knowledge than before. I understand that reading is not for all people, and that being the case, you may have to find another means by which you can gather information daily. In life, we must gather as much information possible in order to act on our ambitions properly and to help other people in following generations act on their ambitions in a way that is most beneficial for the existence of man.

The conversations that we hold with our peers and strangers alike can be utilized to consciously facilitate proper dialogue. The ability to talk in both colloquial and formal diction is of the utmost importance, for you will become more universal, engaging in conversations with people of different backgrounds who may be able to create a connection with you.

Authority figures will be impressed if you can hold a dialogue using formal diction with a coherent understanding of the subject at hand. Likewise, they will also like to see the more fallible aspects of you, for example, talking in slang terms comfortably amongst a peer group.

There is a flip side to this idea, however. If one wishes to antagonize you based on your intellect and syntax, do not talk in a manner that succumbs to the crowd's idealized means of speaking, for you must be your own individual. If the crowd taunts you for using "big words," continue to prove that you are on another level, distinct from the inferior intellect of the group at hand. Be your own. People will wish to hold you within their preconceived parameters that they have created for you when they thought you were "ordinary," but you must break through these barriers.

Nobody will ever be able to pigeonhole you into a notion of intelligence that they have created for you. Aim to live an ambiguous life. Hold the conviction that when you die, nobody will be able to understand the depths of you. If people were not there for you when you were learning, tirelessly aiming to be at the top of your profession, then why would they deserve to understand the knowledge that you possess in its entirety?

Another aspect of existence that is quite telling of an individual's wisdom is if they are seekers of truth. Regardless of belief, Jesus got it right when he said, "And ye shall know the truth, and the truth shall make you free" (John 8:32, KJV). Seeking truth in all aspects of life, even in the most trivial of situations, will allow you to find the tendencies of the people you come across as well as the situations that you are placed into. Aim to be truthful in all situations, for deception is one of the most immoral practices that one can perpetrate against another.

If you wish to rise up in a company or other such career quickly and effectively, your best bet would be to stay true to yourself while also being truthful to all those who surround you. If being truthful to others means that there is a chance you could lose money, then so be it; money does not define you.

The age we live in today is not comparable to any other age we have lived in before. The onset of the technological wave, including social media and artificial intelligence, has left us with a job market entirely different from the one that existed even twenty years ago. It is quite likely that a handful of people from Generation Z will end up working jobs that did not exist when they were born. This leaves us with a major problem, especially since the way educators teach students has not undergone any rapid changes. With an influx of technology-based jobs coming into the economy, traditional education will not cut it anymore. Generation Z must become knowledgeable about all aspects of life, for the school system is surely not going to teach them something of any use unless they seek out courses pertaining to technology and computer science.

Knowledge is key to everything in this world, and we must not let the education system of the 1950s hold us back from becoming the innovators of the future.

As I have become increasingly knowledgeable throughout the years, primarily due to my observations of the people around me, I have come to the realization that everybody we come across is of some value to us. Even those of whom we despise the most are still of an incalculable amount of value, perhaps more so than people we like. The importance of gaining knowledge from those who oppose your views/actions will allow you to get a better grasp on how the world truly functions. By fully understanding this idea, one will eventually learn that knowledge is something that derives from all things.

Seek to become as knowledgeable as possible, for we will never be able to accomplish the feat of becoming all-knowing; that must be left in the hands of the transcendent deity. Gain wisdom from the people around you, and never cease to engage in dialogues and civil discourses with the people that surround you. The people around us hold more knowledge than we think because, obviously, one's outward appearance is not telling of their intellect. Be flexible, and find all of the things in this world that are shrouded in mystery. The truth is going to be hidden in things that we would have never thought possible beforehand.

It is also a near certainty of life that people are going to avoid telling you their "inner" truth at all costs. However, I think this is a good thing. There are some thoughts that are better left without a physical action taken. For instance, sometimes when driving at a high speed, people will think about the repercussions of crashing into a tree, when in reality this would be intrinsically foolish. In this sense, the thought would not be commonly told to other people, for they might write you off as psychotic or for having a proclivity for self-inflicted harm.

Nobody knows you. They think they understand you, but they truly do not have the slightest insight into the depths of your being. Make sure you keep it this way. It is necessary to spread your knowledge to others, but do not allow them to understand your thoughts, for your thoughts define you; they are part of your conscious identity.

You are enveloped within a network, and not all the ideas that are told to us are intended to help us find the truth; they are told to us so that those in power can push narratives upon the powerless teenagers of the twenty-first century. Listen to all the ideas that are spread around, and decipher which ones are of the highest degree of truth. You hold the key to discovering what "is."

Through all the tragedy and suffering that we are subjected to in this world, there is a wide-reaching amount of knowledge at our fingerprints. Part of the importance in understanding that life is destined to have tendencies of both virtue and evil in different dimensions is that we become more enlightened individuals from this understanding of the natural world, its phenomena, and inhabitants that possess the power to doom the world to damnation at any point in time. Nothing is important in this world except for the knowledge gathered by an individual in hopes of spreading a beneficial existence for the generations to come. Your actions and the reasoning behind said actions are more important than conceivable at the time being. Behind every thought resonates the knowledge of prior generations and the fate of future generations. Ideas are most commonly shown through the portrayal of words; this is part of the reasoning behind having free-speech legislation. It would be reprehensible to prohibit an individual from saying words simply because another person was offended or "hurt" by the words being said.

It is beyond doubt that words can incite violence. Using this argument in order to provide a justification as to why some words should be prohibited from being said is entirely telling of a simple-minded individual. Just as words can incite violence, words have the power to unite people and bring about a revolution. In all created things—especially language—there will be forms of virtue and malevolence due to man imposing his will upon all of his creations. This is part of what's wrong behind the idea of "hate speech." Why would we ever allow a governing power to determine what "hate" means? The government should never have the power to dictate what an individual willingly says. We are responsible for the things we say, but we are liable for their effects on the people, not how the government interprets them.

Hurtful words are always said and will continue to be said due to the opinionated nature of the listener. It is up to the people to become more knowledgeable in order to see the inherent dangers in treating people with prejudice. The moment we spread knowledge, not as an educational chore but as an end-goal in life, will be the only moment when we will notice any lasting change in the way people treat each other. The actions of man will remain constant until our demise, although we can change our outlook as to how we interpret phenomena around us. The more knowledge we have, the more aware we become, and the more aware we become, the better fit we are for life.

Chapter 15

The Pursuit of Happiness

HAPPINESS IS SOMETHING THAT IS BEST pursued only when we have found meaning. For some, it is not difficult to find what is meaningful in life. For a handful of others, the search for meaning is a constant scavenger hunt, rendering some individuals unable to find a sustainable means of happiness. I do believe happiness is destined for all of us, but I do not think it is the only necessary thing to attribute to well-being in life.

Second only to meaning, I do believe that the pursuit of happiness is one of the greatest justifications as to why we should live. Finding happiness in this world is the ultimate effort of our existence. We are born into a world knowing that death is inevitable, that suffering will loom around every corner, and malevolence constantly finds a way to inhabit itself within the lives of people. To be able to discover and hold on to happiness in this world is the ultimate test of the human psyche.

The human condition is littered with dichotomies—malevolence and virtue, dark and light, cold and warm. Being able to clear up the inherent confusion with the differentiated nature of existence is telling of an individual's ability to obtain something of greater value in this world, often the case, this being happiness.

Happiness is a beautiful thing and as one who is prone to loneliness, I can tell you that happiness needs to be shared with others. Otherwise, you will become a lesser being than you ought to be. There is no reason why we should seek living at a level of existence less than our potential. One of the biggest flaws I have found in myself is that I have a proclivity to enjoying being alone rather than being in the company of other people. Although I am happy being alone, I have noticed that associating with others in a proper manner leaves me thankful for leaving the confines of my own company. Fully understanding this, I have been able to orient my life in a way that will allow me to become a greater being than the person as whom I have always lived.

We should always aim to live a life of the highest degree possible. This idea is up to many interpretations, depending on the individual, although, in my experience, this particularly has to do with meaning-based happiness. Meaning-based happiness is the most true form of happiness within the human psyche.

It is too often seen that individuals flee to the immediate pleasantries that are associated with substances. We live in a world of instant gratification, and many people would rather feel the quick experience of being disoriented than deal with their problems. It is not the case that drinking, smoking, etc., will make us happy. The contrary is true; they do not make us happy but rather postpone the suffering to a later date. Perhaps drinking alcohol is a prime example of the nature of the world. When we indulge within the comforts of expedient distraction from life, we become free from worry only to feel the repercussions of our ill-advised choice the next day. You can always postpone your issues, but eventually, they will catch up to you, and as a result, you will be confronted by a greater buildup of issues than you thought conceivable in the first instance. In order to become happy, we must stress the importance of manifesting our existence in a means that is most beneficial to our sustenance. Earlier in the book, I discussed the importance of pondering the best of and worst courses of actions to take from your own interpretation of virtue and evil. Confining one's life to ultimate metaphysical parameters will allow one to direct one's life onto the path of greatest value. In this sense, vices such as controlled substances are roadblocks to attaining higher consciousness, an idea in psychology pertaining to the best an individual can be within the human condition. Human beings are powerful beyond our comprehension, but it is our own vices that make it so that we fall short of becoming suitable individuals through the eyes of our own identity.

I also believe that "love," through the comprehension

of youthful minds, is often a vice that blocks one from acting on one's ability to obtain happiness. People are often blind to the fact that the love they experienced in a prior relationship will likely be reconstituted in a different form later on. For this reason, they continue to worry about the uncontrollable. Do not allow your belief that there was something you could have done to make the situation better get in the way of you manifesting a future-self of greater value than before. There is no use in telling someone you miss them if you genuinely know they do not miss you back. If we hold the belief that we have found something of greater value than we experienced in the past, even though we still are preoccupied with a prior relationship, then we are at a stalemate, with no room to persist. We must break off the toxic aspects of our existence. The love that we continue to devote to those who give us no indication of reciprocation will only come back to haunt us, especially in an instance where we have found another person to give our time to. Reserving feelings for your ex-lover will not allow you to love a later significant other with a full heart, leading to a two-sided lie, for you swear to them that you love them even when you do not love them fully, while the other individual swears that they know you even when you have been lying to them the entire time.

As clichéd as it may sound, loving yourself is one of the most important things you can possibly do. Embodied within the idea of loving yourself is the idea of having respect for your identity, respect for who you truly are. It is true that a person can survive on their own, but they cannot thrive on their own. With that said, there are some people who can impose toxic elements upon your existence that are not needed. Because the majority of us are weak when it comes to blocking out "toxic" elements implemented upon us, it is often best to evaluate all the people in our lives to find out where we can pursue our best means of living. Those who are able to deal with negative people generally well should learn from the aspects that they are lacking to learn how to coexist with someone who does not bring about any value. Few people are able to interact and learn from negative people, although those who can may find it valuable to understand the tendencies of as many different people as possible.

Do not let your proclivity to be accepted by all people keep you from being the best possible version of yourself. In all likelihood, it may be best for you to let go of the chance of once again being accepted by a person you interacted with in the past. This discovery will lead you toward the path of happiness, although it may not be experienced at first. After understanding your worth with respect to those around you, the understanding of where you can find happiness can be obtained.

But what is happiness? It is not what you thought it was. You thought happiness was something that only the few experienced when you were wallowing in your own self-pity. Happiness is defined by the individual and only the individual. The masses cannot define what happiness is, because then it is of a dogmatic design. Happiness is not meant to be absolute; it varies upon perspective and experience.

Through television dramas and works of fiction, we are taught that happiness is closely correlated to love. Surely, they are correlated, but true love is also greatly evident when happiness has died. Love is strongest when hell reigns over the individual, crippling them to a point of immense suffering and a person is there to help. In that sense, you cannot write off love as being of happiness. Love is most evident along despair, agony, and suffering.

Happiness is open to the interpretation of the individual, the being, the self. No external force must be able to influence the definition of happiness without the consent of the individual. This idea of conscious consent is the idea of an individual only allowing themselves to stray from their identity if it is for the betterment of their inner being. One's course of action is not always the correct means of operation, and thus, it may be important to do things that do not coincide with the preconceived notion of identity-related phenomena. You can change the way you act, and it is often necessary to do so. The flipside to this is that it will take an immeasurable sacrifice to do so. It is not easy to act out of one's identity because by definition this implies the idea of neglecting the will to act according to the individual's own naturally occurring idiosyncrasies and tendencies.

The peaks of happiness after finding a sustainable sense of meaning will become omnipresent if one's life is oriented in a manner that allows for such a thing. Being open to all experiences may allow you to be happy even despite the terrible experiences you have encountered. However, this may be a troubling route to follow, as you will not be taken seriously in the respect of caring for your dignity or the well-being of others.

Your image should never become the exact replica of what your inner life truly is. In this respect, it is best to be humble—being happy on the inside without being overly ecstatic on the outside. To many, the image is what people often like best about the individual, rather than the sides that are hidden from the outer world. Perhaps this is as it should be, but it is also likely that someone who cares too much about their image will be lost in times of existential crisis. The best bet would be to realize that your image and inner-self are two radically different things and that you are in control of the degree of disparity, although it is often best to refrain from allowing people to know every secret you hold within your mind.

I have never bought into the idea that a smile accurately reflects one's inner emotions. You can be unequivocally happy without feeling the need to smile. In the same way, even those who show a smile can be severely depressed, as is seen in the case of many celebrities. Regardless, it is important to realize how your body language may affect the people around you.

People are fragile and susceptible to trauma and perhaps putting on a smile can make someone indirectly moved by means of associative happiness.

It is important to aim to always have meaningful days in order to create a sense of happiness in oneself. Getting up early in the morning for school was always a struggle for me. Besides the fact that I was a firm critic of the notion that school was "essential," I simply dreaded the idea of getting up early in the morning when I was up until midnight the previous night, working on homework. Fixing this issue was quite simple for me. The only way to alleviate the dread of waking up early in the morning was to find a means of enjoying myself, which was almost always finding some means of having a purposeful day. The solution to such an issue could be looking forward to speaking to a pretty girl, learning from a teacher who I saw as a mentor, or engaging in social interactions with those attempting to challenge my intellect. It is not always expedient to act like you want to be somewhere when you are fully aware, deep down, that you truly do not. However, great lessons are learned when you do things that you do not have the slightest desire to do, either because they are agonizing or because they do not make you happy. I promise you that if you find something meaningful in the events that make you unhappy, the repercussions of your persistence will formulate uniquely oriented happiness later on in your life.

Human emotions can be radically different

experiences from one individual to another. However, one constant means of experiencing happiness is to accept the beauty that lies within the world. Take time to examine architecture such as cathedrals, skyscrapers, and houses. With all art, people spend an invaluable amount of time on the things they are passionate about. Look at works of architecture as a means of understanding what it means to live a purposeful existence. Cathedrals and places of religious worship are decorated with mosaic and stained glass to draw in the eyes of onlookers with their beauty. Beauty and happiness are closely correlated. When seeing a beautiful girl, a breathtaking piece of art, or a violently intriguing ocean, this is where happiness may be found. Even in the most devastating of things, beauty resonates. Beauty is up to interpretation, as the common expression has held for centuries. Do not be one who neglects to accept the beauty that lies within life. Yes, life is, to a large degree, suffering—as the religions have preached for millennia—but there is beauty lying in even the most gruesome things.

To the eyes of the terrestrial human, the ocean is a place of destruction and chaos. This is not the truth, and the terrestrial being holds the wrong convictions. Perhaps one could have a better attitude regarding the ocean if they understood that 80 percent of all life on earth stems from the ocean. Being of selfish character, the human neglects to realize that he is not so dissimilar from the beings of the ocean, for in the end, life is life.

Not having an emotional or physical attachment to the oceans, the human dumps his fecal matter and harmful waste into the ocean so that he does not have to deal with it, not considering that this would be like defecating upon one's neighbor's lawn. We are all beings. We all live. Although our notions of the world are drastically different, our advancements have only allowed us to lose sight of the similarities between us. I do believe we would be happier beings if we learned to live in unison rather than live as selfish beings. There needs to be more love in the world. People often find meaning by identifying the importance of love. If we could make it culturally acceptable to continually show love for people, regardless of whether they are strangers or not, the world would be a much better place. Unfortunately, we may never be able to see such a world. Utopia is likely impossible, and even if one were established, the natural course of free will would probably damn it all to hell. However, the faith that there is a chance that people are going to be better humans to each other, through care and love, is an idea that keeps me from losing my sense of moral credence.

Happiness is something that is destined for all of us, and I really believe that notion to be true. There is no point in living if one is not able to find happiness at some point in one's life. Once meaning has been found, I would advocate that you put yourself in the position to experience as much happiness as you possibly can. Life is brutal, and one of the only means to counteract that brutality is to position ourselves to be happy even in our most vulnerable areas.

There is a reason for everything; never think that your problems are unique to you. The pursuit of happiness will constantly be postponed because of issues that come about in our lives, but you must never let these issues stop you from obtaining the happiness you so desperately need. In time, all things will subside, including your own happiness; however, like all things, the experience will be reconstituted again and often in a more enriching form, when one has found meaning. This is the normal course of events in the world, and we must accept this doctrine to hold truth. Terrible things are destined to happen to us, but it is not the case that only terrible things will enter our life. Suffering may vary in every life, but our awareness of the world, as well as our identity, will allow us to experience beneficial things, such as happiness.

You will experience a lot of hurt in this world—death, heartbreak, etc. However, you will see many beautiful things in this world as well. It is the same hurtful experiences in life that make beautiful things much more valuable. This idea should bring you comfort, maybe even happiness, for it is not guaranteed you will wake up tomorrow. Dedicate your life to the pursuit of commodities that best suit your existence in this world, and you will likely experience happiness.

Having lost people that meant a great deal to me helped me understand the importance of life. Life—that is, in the sense of the human condition—embodies all things. With happiness, there is immense suffering. With virtue, there is evil. With the rational, there is the irrational. With existence, there is death. With black, there is white. Through this understanding, life is a collection of binary experiences. Dichotomies. Understanding these dichotomies as well as the need for them will point you in the direction of truth, hopefully even meaning. If we have lived naturally, free will will take care of us to the degree that we will likely find meaning within the nature of opposites.

We have been given a great opportunity to build a life full of meaning. Do not mess up your chances of ensuring that your life is productive. You are a contractor that must create the blueprints for your own home (life). You will find happiness, but you will need to build up a sturdy foundation to ultimately obtain this happiness. The stairs will creak, and the paint on the walls will chip, but these things are only the most trivial of things when the home you have created has a sturdy foundation with a beautiful view.

There is much to see in this world of endless views. Be able to take every situation, every experience, every image for what it is. In the end, there truly is a meaning to all things. A purposeless existence is only an idea that humans have brought about through nihilistic philosophies. In fact, it is these same philosophies that result in a state of selfishness. For the holder of the belief that life is purposeless does not account for every other being on this planet, besides the human being. They do not take into consideration that a flower pollinates in order to reproduce and create offspring. If the flower itself did not have a purpose, it would cease to exist. The followers of the false indoctrination of purposelessness would also not be particularly fond of the idea that the heart beats in order to circulate blood throughout the body, thus giving it a purpose.

The greatest enemy of man is himself. His ideas deceive him into thinking that he is a lesser being, put into a lesser world full of lesser experiences. In reality, the opposite is true. For we are put into a world where the only guarantee is death, although we are able to find beauty in the most frightening of things. It is through man's eternal wisdom that he has subjected himself to the most suffering. As man holds the conviction that he has become wiser, he holds false rationalizations in regards to how the world is "supposed" to work.

It is often the case that people confuse the word serious with the word static. To be serious does not mean to block out everything that is in the way of one's thinking. The very nature of the world is serious, for it is real. To truly be serious means to experience happiness, find meaning, enjoy oneself, and love others, all while being able to focus on a common goal. Being serious and having tunnel vision are entirely different ideas. It is sometimes mistakenly thought that having tunnel vision is a good way of pursuing a course of action. Although it may be beneficial to narrow your sights in regards to what you are aiming for, more likely, if you have tunnel vision, you will be unaware of something occurring in your periphery that may be meaningful to you. Your life must be a meaningful dedication to every course of action you embark upon. Part of what is correlated within the idea of being "meaningful" is to be aware of the things that are occurring around you, regardless if that means you must sacrifice a certain aspect of your life.

Pursuing happiness after making a great sacrifice or after experiencing an unprecedented amount of suffering is one of the biggest struggles that an untrained individual may come across in life. Perhaps to put it simply, one of the best philosophies on embarking on an adventurous course of action such as this would be to sell yourself into the belief that the things that occur to you in life do not happen despite you. They happen so that you can grow into a being that is the best possible version of yourself.

Finding the best possible version of yourself is a genuinely confusing idea. However, the confusion is exactly the point. The reason why it confuses us is that we have no comprehension of what the best possible version of ourselves may look like. This is the same as trying to explain the color blue to a blind man. Having no comprehension of what color looks like, the argument seems purposeless. However, the blind man still knows that colors exist, because he holds the conviction that what he is being told is of some amount of truth. In this respect, why is it so hard for us to imagine a version of ourselves we have never seen before? Belief is hard for people because it is not something that can be seen. When one learns to believe, whether in religion, the structure of the world, or in the fact that things may just get better for them in the future, they will establish a strong foundation for the road toward happiness.

It is beneficial to take responsibility for your life. It is beyond important to take responsibility for all the good and bad things that occur, as well as for doing what you are required to do. We must own up to every single aspect of our life. In the end, the terrible things we endure are still a part of us and we must have a certain amount of respect toward the suffering we have endured. We are molded through experience, and the person you are today is better off because of the things that you have endured. Find happiness in knowing that your life is going to have to be a continual comeback story, for that is truly the nature of existence.

Do the things that you need to do to be better off in the future. Sometimes we feel that we cannot move on to manifest something greater in our life because we are being held back by someone. It is likely the case that sacrificing the relations you have with the person will hurt them. However, it would hurt them a lot more if they found out that you were not living a fulfilling life.

Remember that life is meant to be enjoyed. There is no reason to go on living in a manner where you hate the mere fact of existing. There is a better world waiting for you when you take the time to appreciate all of what makes this life meaningful and worth living. Your life is important, my friend. Never let anyone—especially your negative self-thinking—dictate whether your life is important. Your existence matters in this world, my friend. Never forget that. You will always be loved. I promise you that happiness is going to come your way.

1-800-273-8255

Chapter 16

Defense/Coping Mechanisms

PEOPLE HIDE WITHIN CERTAIN PERSONAS as a means of protecting themselves from the harsh realities that they come across throughout the natural course of events in the world. It is not bad to have these sorts of defense mechanisms, although it is important to recognize how such a means of living can cripple us from pursuing something of greater importance and stop us from obtaining a goal.

Growing up as a particularly shy kid, I often hid within the confines of my room. Many fear being locked within the confines of a room for hours on end, but for me, there was something comforting about being alone. When I was alone, I could work on things that made me happiest, and I could imagine things without the fear of others telling me that what I was thinking was irrational. Using loneliness as a defense mechanism to counteract my fear of social interaction, I was able to gradually discover what was most important to me over the accumulation of years.

Seeing the faults in the ways that other people treated me, I was able to create a basis for how I would later pursue interactions with others. As high school came, I became increasingly more social, although it took great effort to do so. Even now, as much as I enjoy interacting with groups of people, there is something comforting that I find in my solitude. Relations with other people led me to see the absolute worst in people while occasionally seeing that few people did enjoy caring and loving for others.

After experiencing a bit of suffering through relationships, as well as through the loss of people close to my heart, the social aspect of me, the part that interacted with as many people as possible, became more of a facade for something that was hiding within me. Depression claimed a foothold within my mind after the suffering I had faced, easily doing so due to my proclivity to be alone. The mind can be your worst enemy when you are alone. For me, part of the reason I enjoyed being alone so much was my understanding that people could not hurt me when I was in my lonesome. This idea was gradually debunked as I saw how the depressed human psyche poses a much greater threat to the well-being of an individual than people ever could.

Around this time, I realized that meaning is something that would be genuinely beneficial for my life. At the time, I was simply existing and not living; living is when the spirit of the individual has found a meaningful premise of life in order to find happiness. After a long period of self-discovery and attainment of knowledge, I was able to create a premise upon which I needed to live.

At this time, I finally understood that my desire to be alone was not healthy for me and though I struggle with the idea of being given affection, I was able to own up to this. I was able to grow, and my life changed entirely. It was not that I was susceptible to the suffering that I faced on a constant basis but merely that I had grown to be exceedingly more courageous than before. I understood I was going to be hurt without end for many years but I was also able to understand the fact that this was the most necessary part of living life, for it makes you determine a purpose in life. If you have a purpose for doing things in life, even the most egregious events that unfold before you will become mere trivialities in the scope of what is it that you are looking for.

Thankfully for me, my mechanism of hiding from the suffering I faced in the world was not nearly as self-destructive as that of many of my colleagues I had grown up with. Drugs and alcohol are desirable to many but they only alleviate pain for a couple of hours before you have to come back to the reality of life. Then the cycle repeats and as the pain comes back around you find a means of getting more of the desired substance into your body until one day you wake up getting your stomach pumped, or worse, never waking up.

Perhaps part of the reason why I wanted to write this book was that I saw there was a definitive need for my message to be heard. It is not that my message is any better than anyone else's—for the themes in this book have been written about for centuries—but that I am able to relate to my generation well. I see the inadequacies of Generation Z and I understand how they can be managed.

In the end, I believe all addictions, especially those of a metaphysical nature, must be managed, for if they are not they can lead to much more sinister mechanisms of alleviating pain. It is important to find a means of dealing with all the suffering that exists in life but I genuinely believe that the only proper means to go about doing this is to create a purpose, a reason why you must continue to live, something that will last with you for the rest of your life.

The world is full of many terrible things but it is what we do to counteract these terrible things in a proper manner that will allow us to help others when they are looking for a way out of the pangs of their existence. Aim to help others in everything that you do and it is likely the case that you will be helped out in a later time; call it karma, if you like. The universe has an interesting way of proving to us that our existence is more than arbitrary in nature and I believe this is discovered only through the appreciation for one's fellow man as well as the love that they share for each other.

When people started to believe that such a terrible

world, destined for failure, could not be the creation of a transcendent being they started to run toward the safety that draws one toward atheism. To resist believing in supernatural phenomena is the easy thing to do. In this respect, I draw the conclusion that atheism is a type of defense mechanism (contradictory to the ideas of the brilliant Friedrich Nietzsche). It is not bad to be an atheist; nor is it bad to be a Christian. However, if you harbor within belief or the lack thereof merely as a defense mechanism, then you are entirely wrong. Going back to Nietzsche's ideas of a world comprised of intertwined opposites—though such an idea is not unique to Nietzsche's literature—things are both true and false at the same time, based on perspective. For instance, one may say that God is a lie because no world based on the universal central force of virtue would be quite as evil as it is. At the same time, God can be the greatest truth of all, wherein the kingdom of God is within us and is meant to be revealed based on our interactions with the natural world and the malevolent temptations of man. In much the same way, things can be considered both virtuous and evil based on the intent of the individual. So I ask you the question: If a man catches a woman as she jumps off a building in the hope of committing suicide, only to take money from her pocket, is he virtuous or evil? The answer would be both, for life is one big dichotomy that is manifested in all things.

Just as there is life, there must be death. Just as there is black, there must be white. Just as there is happiness, there must be suffering. Nothing could exist without having a counterpart. And so it is with this notion that I tell you that it would be foolish to hide in the defense mechanism that is embodied within the rejection of belief, for that contradicts the nature of being.

You will experience many vile interactions in this world but never allow this to move you to the point of vice, wherein you hide within the rejection of belief as a defense mechanism. Psychologically, I would not advise you to reject beliefs because chances are you will have a lack of trust in the legitimacy of any possible thing in this world, or any other, for that matter. There is much more to existence than what we can understand rationally. To us, ideas of the unconscious mind, as discussed by Jung, seem irrational; it is only after understanding how things of truth often have a degree of irrationality that we will be able to make sense of the phenomena around us.

Another common defense mechanism individuals use to hide within is treating others with disrespect and nastiness. It is common that a lack of trust in people leads to treating others poorly. Some may feel as if treating others with mean-spiritedness will keep them away from ever entering their life, limiting the likelihood of the individual ever being hurt. This is often the case in those who experience a severe heartbreak, not allowing anybody to talk to them regardless of the newcomer's intentions.

A similar idea is seen in other victims of heartbreak,

wherein they continue to desire the very person who hurt them most. In many ways, this is one of the worst possible coping mechanisms when it comes to trying to handle the grief of the world in its entirety. Desiring the one who hurt you most will only leave you in a disarray, as you are unintentionally reinforcing the fact that you think of yourself as having little value other than what another person places on you. Value is not defined by others. It is defined by the individual. You must understand your own worth and learn to love yourself for who you are. Do not carry on with needless suffering because of the thoughts you cannot get out of your head of when times were once good. Chances are your comprehension of "good" is radically different than the definition the future version of yourself would have. You owe it to yourself to be open to things that are thrust upon you in life; never be certain that the way in which you are living currently is any better than it could ever be. More likely, you are holding a bias in regards to whether you believe you are suitable for the world or whether the way you live might hold a greater amount of substance. It is good to check on your biases in order to ensure that you are pursuing a course of action of best interest.

It is often the case that your bias serves as a defense mechanism in your life. Trying to comprehend the idea that you are inadequate in any dimension serves you to hold bias in the fact wherein you think you are "doing just fine." No, you are not doing just fine, and it is highly likely that something is missing within you even though your persona insists otherwise.

Defense mechanisms are most easily identifiable through an individual's persona. The poet Charles Bukowski understood this quite well.

"Those who preach God, need God."

More often than not, those who pride themselves on a certain aspect of their life need that very thing over everything else. This is entirely telling of an individual's intrinsic defense mechanisms. The things that we harbor closest to us within our identities are the things we cannot live without. In the case of the Bukowski poem excerpt, replace "God" with any other word and the phrase would likely hold as much reasoning as it did before. The case is amplified even more in the use of the word God. This is one of the top issues of our existence in this world. Regardless if one is a believer or not, the phrase holds an incalculable amount of truth.

In theory, anything that holds people from facing the realities of life is a form of a defense mechanism. If only people understood the fact that the suffering endured in the past was only for the betterment of themselves in the future, they would have no need for defense mechanisms. However, it is not clear to me that such an idea is self-evidently true, for people always hesitate to discuss their issues. If they embraced their suffering, then discussing a hurtful past would not be so difficult.

Loss commonly turns people into a form that is entirely inconsistent with their original being. Perhaps

I understand this better than many, having experienced this myself on numerous occasions. When a significant other leaves you, in the respect that they stop loving you, it is not entirely different from that person having passed away. In the end, the heart hurts just as much, only the crying faced with death is more socially acceptable than it is for a breakup. This is why people carry so much pain within them, especially when a relationship comes crashing to the ground. Seeing that person who meant the most to you move on to find someone else, fully knowing that the new person they are with is the same as you in a different form but simply at a "better time", can be scarring. Maybe the part that hurts us to a larger degree is the fact that we do not know what could have been. Similar to when one passes on, we will never know what they could have done given the time to do so.

Experiencing loss early on has a genuinely profound effect on the premature mind. Such examples include an individual's parents divorcing, someone close to them dying, or losing someone who meant a significant amount to them. Often the targets of these forms of suffering tend to hide within defense mechanisms to keep them from the hurt that they believe people are going to impose upon them.

We must rid ourselves of the defense mechanisms that hold us back, the ones that stop us from reaching a greater understanding of the natural phenomena occurring around us. The world is filled with suffering but that must not keep us from reaching a higher state of being than the one that we are presently living within. There is much to see in this world and if our mindsets become roadblocks in the way of experiencing something meaningful, then it may be the right time to make revisions to our mindset.

The only one stopping you from speaking your being into this world is you. Every step you take in this world is a risk. We believe the floor beneath us to be steady ground but there is always the chance that the floor can fall from underneath us in every endeavor we embark upon. With this said, take the time and be genuinely excited about the life that you are going to live. Through all the pain, through all the hurt, there is still beauty and we must look forward to those moments in our life where we experience something that gives us a heightened sense of self-importance, a form of spiritual enlightenment. To liberate the spirit within us, we must be able to keep ourselves free from any blockage in either the physical or metaphysical sense.

It is not always the case that we will be able to keep ourselves heading in the right direction. Going into our negative mindsets is often the easiest thing for us to do and we cannot go about life on our own. The people you surround yourself with often have better insight into some of the issues you are facing because they do not hold any of the internal biases that you hold.

Find a person who makes your existence in this world meaningful. Never let that person go, for they will be a valuable asset in guiding you to finding yourself again. We will always lose our course but someone who can help keep our negative side at bay—while bringing out the positives—is one of the most treasurable influences we may have in this life. We are beings of love. Your past relationships are not justifiable reasons as to why people do not enjoy loving or that people do not need love. Love exists naturally but it is the human elements within us that corrupt the relationship itself. Remembering that love and beauty exist in all things will allow us to stray away from our propensity toward defense mechanisms.

Chapter 17
Make Love a Priority

LOVE IS A GREAT ENERGY THAT FLOWS through all. Love often allows us to see the best of what a course of human undertaking can lead us toward. Perhaps it is this love within us that causes us to do things of a nature that brings about pain and agony. One thing for certain is that love has a drug-like effect on us that can both encourage us and cloud our judgment simultaneously.

Sometimes we love so much that we leave each other broken; what a terrible thing. This must not hamper us from contributing to any course of action that regards moving toward being in a relationship. The very nature of human relations is a thing of immense risk. This is what makes them invaluable. At any moment, the floor beneath us can come crashing down and we can fall into the abyss of heartbreak. There is no guarantee that things will ever last into the future, and this is why it is important to be honest with how you feel about a person when you have the chance, in the likely chance that they never get the opportunity to know how you felt within. People are only temporary but the feelings we share between one another will stand the test of time, for they are reconstituted through the spirits of the people that we are able to touch in this lifetime.

Tell people how you feel about them. Lying to them serves no purpose. If you wish to be with them, then you will find an excuse to be with them rather than find an excuse as to why you could not be with them. It is out of love that we share the most important aspects of the human condition, where things of meaning are most clearly seen.

The unifying qualities of love have direct repercussions along various dimensions of one's life and it is incredibly important to actively involve oneself with the pursuit of love. Heartbreak deters people from loving but this is one of the most critical mistakes one can make. Everybody has the capacity to love—I do believe that. The reason that they refuse to love is due to internal issues resulting from past experiences, which have rendered them handicapped in the department of love and human relation. Humans are born to love, but love does not necessarily mean that they are going to do what is virtuous. People will do whatever is best for their benefit so therein which lies in love is the idea that intention is the primeval cause of misunderstanding.

Sometimes people love to simply keep themselves satisfied in the hopes that they can postpone the problems that they harbor within. Not only is this dangerous, but it is also an instinct of bad intentions because one's counterpart is foolishly falling into a trap, with the floor beneath them certain to fall in the near future. I spoke earlier of expedient relations being used as a defense mechanism for one not having to deal with their own internal chaos. This is a disengagement from the problems that one is carrying within. Due to the individual not dealing with their problems in a proper manner, it is likely that their own problems will be passed along to their significant other, whether it was their intention to do so or not.

Love is a game of risk. To be in love means to be equally loved as one loves another. In this sense, it is one of the greatest gambles one can make. The condition of being stems from this love. The religions of the world are based upon the love that God brings to the lives of his followers.

People often confuse their sexuality with their love life. The ideas are entirely different and though they do have a slight bit of overlap, it is not the case that love is non-existent without sex. In teenagers, this idea is commonly misinterpreted. People are readily willing to abandon those who sacrifice the most for them simply due to the fact that their sexual desires are not able to be acted upon.

Love is an act of faith. A sense of oneness with the

person who brings about the highest degree of meaning and purpose to your life. In this sense, if you are in a relationship and you are not genuinely moved by the person as if they bring a greater meaning to the world for you, it is likely the case that you are not truly in love with the person but rather in lust with them; in love with the idea of them.

When loving someone, it is important to love them without strangling them. That is to say, just as a small child loves a furry animal so much that it squeezes it to the point that it is asphyxiated. It is important to realize that love between two people does not have to be physically expressed in order for the love to exist. Physical expression is only a reassurance that the love exists but when it becomes all that exists within a relationship, one's significant other may become strangled, unable to act on their will as they choose. You must allow the person that you love to love themselves just as much as they may be loved by you.

Fear of abandonment causes people to go into relations with a feeling of being unwilling to love. They believe that halfway entering a course of human undertaking will keep them from becoming too attached when the time comes when they are abandoned by the person that they have dedicated their time to. This is the wrong model. If you are only semi-invested in a relationship because you are afraid of being hurt, then you are only pushing the suffering induced by heartbreak to a later date, when it is likely the case that you were finally willing to love someone. What you put into this world will come back to haunt you at another time, for better or worse.

We owe it to ourselves to love fully. There is too much hatred and suffering in the world to only give half of your heart to the people around you. As much as it may seem that others are annoyed by you, it is likely the case that they are dealing with internal issues and they have no other option but to block out any other distractions. Be willing to help these people with every ounce of love in your heart in hopes that when you are at a time of crisis in your life there will be someone else there to look out for you.

Pop culture fantasizes over love and it is not without reason. People live because of love. Those who do not have love in their hearts are merely existing on a speck of dust in an infinite universe. It is through love that we have faith, hope, and embodiments of divine belief. One of the few instances that I would advocate following the will of the crowd would be through the prioritization of love. With that said, allow your love to be unique to you, and by this pathway you will experience a love similar only to the identities of you and the significant other that you are targeting.

Loving on the basis of your needs and your partners' needs will make it so that your relationship is less likely to be dismantled by external forces beyond your control. Never aim to please other people by looking as if you are the perfect couple. Nothing can ever be statistically perfect. The things that are perfect are only in such a way because they are yet to be disproven. If you aim to look like the poster child for what a good relationship should look like, it is highly likely that you are not targeting the internal needs between you and your partner. Relationships are founded upon reciprocity. What you give to me, I give to you, and vice versa.

You must prioritize the mutual assertion of each other's needs in order to bring your relationship to a level where both partners are getting the absolute most out of the other. People say they are afraid of love because they do not have a proper means of comparison to what a beneficial relationship should look like. Too often, these people live in the past, for they do not understand that the past is merely trivial. We have to live for now. Now is always occurring. It is impossible to reach the past and change things, for better or worse.

Have the attitude that now is the time for you to do what it is that you need to do in order to become the best possible version of yourself. I define this principle as being the supreme form of self-love. If we live for now, then we will surely stray from disappointment when the time comes that we experience suffering. Having this mindset will only further reinforce the fact that the struggles you face are only so that the events that you experience in the future are meaningful and joyous.

Live for now. There is no way of retreating back into our former ways of living, especially when that refers to relationships. Seek the reciprocity that is embodied within love—the mutual assertion of the needs of another. The people in your life that are willing to sacrifice and care for you to the point of embarrassment and disappointment on behalf of others are the ones that love you more than anyone else in this world. You would be foolish to abandon a person as such. Make it your goal to surround yourself with people who are going to show you what it means to genuinely be loved.

The greatest mindset to have in regards to self-love: there is no better time than now. This idea will show your body that you are not willing to cooperate with it and that your mind is stronger than the will within you to quit. To truly love yourself means that you are unwilling to allow any aspect of your being to be subject to any form of negative principles. With that said, as with all values in life, they are up to you to determine. As you have created guidelines of morality upon which to live, you must also create guidelines upon which you will maintain physical and psychological well-being.

Create standards upon which you will always strive to meet, and it is likely you will always be in search of something in life. Perhaps this is the greatest condition of life, always being in search of a better life. Although you should respect where you are in life—as well as the sacrifices it has taken to get there—it is important never to be pleased. Search for something greater. Creating an omnipresent force of discovery is the ultimate force of self-love.

The relationship you hold with yourself is the most

important relationship you will ever hold in this life. If you do not have a strong relationship with yourself, you will never be able to actively contribute to the lives of those around you. The prioritization of the love you have for yourself will lead to a manifestation in love for others. Self-love is the primordial will toward love for those who surround you—a pay-it-forward type deal.

When you are given the opportunity to love someone, accept the challenge and love fully. There is no time to waste in life; every little bit of time we are given must be utilized toward a meaningful pursuit of human undertaking. Never waste the chance to be with someone that will change your understanding of what it means to be alive. When we meet a person who genuinely loves us—rather than takes advantage of us—they change the meaning of the word being, from existing to living. The fire within our hearts lights up once again, like a candle being lit at the end of a dark corridor.

We will soon be dead and the opportunity for us to carry on our love is through the hearts of those we have loved. Love is a great energy and when one gives the gift of love to another they are able to carry that love on as if it were of a tangible nature. The most valuable of all things is love and the love that we experience is a reconstituted form of the love passed down from those who lived generations before us.

If someone close to you passes away, it is your obligation to pass on the love that they held within their hearts and shared with others. Similarly, when a relationship ends, it is important to remember the beneficial aspects of the relationship—given the chance that there was a beneficial aspect—so that you can learn and adapt into a person who knows how to love through conditioning and mutual assertion of needs.

Never forget that your love is one of the most valuable currencies you could ever give to someone. The sacrifice that is associated with love shows others that you are willing to give up a part of yourself in the off chance that you may end up being successful in your efforts of reaching a form of human relationship that is worthwhile. People want to be loved. Love is a type of euphoria, quite similar to that associated with substance use.

Love is a reciprocation. In a healthy relationship, the work we put in is equal to the benefits that we will receive. Having a basic understanding of the reciprocating nature of love will give you a greater insight into the conditions of life along all dimensions. Life is a network of games, all requiring a certain amount of risk. Love acts as the easiest analogy to understanding other aspects of life because it is something that we all have a basic comprehension of. People are inherently born with a comprehension of love, as seen through the longing for a baby to be near his mother.

Reciprocation exists in all forms of human effort. However, not everything has as proportional of a relationship as does that which is seen through sharing love with another person. The reciprocal nature that is seen through human connection is simply the easiest to understand on the basis of effort, and that is the primary reason that I use it as a means of understanding the world as a whole. It is easier to teach people philosophies on life when they have a basic understanding of what you are talking about.

My friend, one of the most important things you can do in this world is to find a love for existence. Once you are able to have a love for existence, you will have a love for yourself and all of that which exists in this world. At this point, you will learn how to truly live life. Through all of the tragedies you face in life, the love and respect you hold for the nature of existence will keep you hopeful that you are exactly where you should be in this world. Your life is not purposeless and you must find a means to have deep respect, perhaps even a love for such an idea. Keep being you.

Epilogue

THE PURPOSE OF WRITING THIS BOOK WAS not to boost my standing in this world but rather to discuss some of the pivotal issues that I believe must be targeted in order to bring about a meaningful existence in this world. I do not feel as if prior generations have done a good job to help Generation Z with the problems that they face.

Generation Z has likely been given the greatest amount of equal opportunities to bring about success, more so than any generation before. With that said, with great opportunity comes great responsibility and one of the biggest issues that Generation Z faces is the fact that they have been placed in a world of instant gratification without having been taught how to take responsibility for the world that is before them. Not having any insight into how to properly take responsibility for both the tragedies and fortunes that they have been given,

Generation Z hides within their artificial selves, the ones that exist within the phone itself. The artificial aspect of our identities has become our persona. On social media, we show only the elements that we want people to see, while the issues that need to truly be targeted are still harbored within, not being properly dealt with.

I do not believe that there is something that can be defined as the perfect advice. The interpretation of advice varies on how the individual chooses to receive the information that is bestowed upon them. This book is merely a collection of the ideas that I have acquired as a result of discovering who I truly am and who I am in relation to the world. Regardless of the advice, the best bet is to listen, in the hopes that you will learn something of value. Truly, this is the reason behind writing this book.

This last year of my life has been one of the hardest endeavors that I have ever embarked upon. In this year, I experienced the most severe depression of my life, I dealt with the loss of many people close to me, and I endured severe heartbreak. Through it all, I grew as an individual and learned that my existence in this world has a meaning behind it. Perhaps I have not yet discovered it, but the pursuit of this meaning is what has given me a heightened sense of self-importance. Life has chewed me up and spit me out but I have always refused to quit because I have been in search of something greater. I am not yet proud of the man I am, although I am proud of the man that I am becoming. This book is a testimony to my will to search for something of greater importance.

Now, as to you, my friend, it is your turn. It is your time to pursue something of greater importance. There is much to this world and with that, it means that there is much for you to discover, much for you to fix, and much for you to learn about. Never forget your importance in this world. The people around you need you much more than you can quite possibly reason out, for you will never entirely know how someone feels about you. Place this last piece of advice close to your heart, and you will never fail to disappoint yourself. Always remember: keep being you.

Printed in the United States
By Bookmasters